Naomi Janowitz
Acts of Interpretation

Religion and Reason

Founded by Jacques Waardenburg (†)

Edited by
Gustavo Benavides, Michael Stausberg,
and Ann Taves

Volume 66

—

Semiotics of Religion

Edited by
Massimo Leone, Fabio Rambelli, and Robert Yelle

Volume 7

Naomi Janowitz

Acts of Interpretation

Ancient Religious Semiotic Ideologies
and Their Modern Echoes

DE GRUYTER

ISBN 978-3-11-135789-8
e-ISBN (PDF) 978-3-11-076860-2
e-ISBN (EPUB) 978-3-11-076862-6
ISSN 0080-0848

Library of Congress Control Number: 2021953517

Bibliographic information published by the Deutsche Nationalbibliothek
The Deutsche Nationalbibliothek lists this publication in the Deutsche Nationalbibliografie;
detailed bibliographic data are available on the Internet at http://dnb.dnb.de.

www.degruyter.com

For Noah and Gideon

Acknowledgments

Earlier versions of Chapter One appeared in *Signs and Society* 6; of Chapter Two in Robert Yelle, Courtney Handman, and Christopher Lehrich (eds.), *Language and Religion,* and Jenny Ponzo, Robert A. Yelle, and Massimo Leone (eds.), *Mediation and immediacy: A key issue for the semiotics of religion*; and of Chapter Five in Jason van Boom and Thomas-Andreas Põder (eds.), *Sign, Method, and the Sacred: New directions in semiotic methodologies for the study of religion.*

I would like to thank Richard Parmentier, Cale Johnson, Flagg Miller, Seth Sanders, Courtney Handman, Robert Yelle, Nancy Felson, Archana Venkatesan, Jenny Ponzo, and the late Michael Silverstein. I would also like to thank Kenton Goldsby, Aron Tillema, and Roberto Delgadillo for research support, Juliana Froggatt, Paul Psonios and Jonathan Grayson for copy editing, and my writing partner Ulrike Strasser.

Contents

Introduction: Explaining and Misunderstanding How Signs Work

Everyone who uses words has ideas about how language works. The Kalapalo of Brazil emphasize the deceptive capacity of language, since the speaker may be lying (Basso 1987). For the Maring, words can be a "means of disguising the true intentionality of an actor" (LiPuma 2000, 164). Words may speak louder than deeds, or, as in the Genesis creation story, words may become deeds. Words may pale in comparison to the exchange of gifts, which can be a better route to knowing someone's internal states (Strathern 1981, 301).

Ideas about words, referred to as in this study as a linguistic ideology, influence every aspect of culture.[1] These shared ideas are the basis that permits the creation of culture, one linguistic event at a time. At the same time, a linguistic ideology cannot easily be transformed into an abstract model for the study of, for example, ritual or religion. Speakers do not fully understand what they are doing when they use language. They cannot fully articulate what they are doing when they use words. Simply put, language often influences speakers in ways that they are not aware of (Lucy 1992). As Michael Silverstein has pointed out in a series of foundational articles, these ideologies are based on a partial awareness that speakers have about the multifunctionality of language and how it encodes truths about the world. Silverstein explains, "The conscious native-speaker's sense of the transparency of the universe to representation by one's own language, and perhaps to language in general, is a function of (a) language's fashions of speaking, through which the universe makes itself manifest to the speaker and which thus guide the conscious, common sense of the representational systems" (2000, 99).

Ideas about language influenced ancient understandings of everything from divinity to truth. These ideas are also the basis for the models used in the modern study of religion. The recycling of ancient ideas is not always made explicit, because models drawn from language appear to simply reveal the nature of whatever aspect of culture is being modeled. Three brief examples help clarify this point. First, Lakoff and Johnson (1980) argue that metaphors exert a specific impact on cognitive functions. Their influential study is based on a narrow and historically specific concept of metaphor. Metaphors, contra Lakoff and Johnson, are not necessarily universal, nor is everything they characterize as a metaphor

---

1 For the term "linguistic ideology," see Silverstein (1979 and 1998).

https://doi.org/10.1515/9783110768602-001

equivalent (Johnson 2017, 75).[2] As Cale Johnson writes about Lakoff and Johnson, "Their focus on the ARGUMENT IS WAR metaphor is really a kind of ethnography and, indeed, a meta-commentary on present-day academic disputes" (Johnson 2017, 75). We learn a great deal about how academics construct their arguments but less about the tremendous cross-cultural variation in the use and meaning of all sorts of pseudo-definitions.

Second, Silverstein's analysis (2000) of Benedict Anderson's work on the "imagined community of the modern nation" provides another example of a linguistic model that is utilized but not fully accounted for. Anderson laid bare the particular "we" voicing of the modern newspaper used to create a presumed community of readers. He relies on language for the "supernatural order of collective consciousness" (Silverstein 2000, 10). Anderson problematically shifted from "reading from one particular resulting discursive linguistic form, objective realist reportage, with its particular deictic presuppositions, to project therefore a whole homogeneous cultural order of subjectivity" (Silverstein 2000, 124). Anderson is inadvertently demonstrating Whorf's point, that language supplies the models for reality in ways that speakers have no awareness of.[3] Any linguistic model must become part of a hardscrabble causal chain supported by very real power in order to make one voice dominate others.

Our third example highlights how hard it is to avoid recycling a linguistic ideology into a theory of ritual or even a model for truth. Roy Rappaport's influential study of religion addressed the issues of efficacy specifically through the lens of Peircean terminology (Rappaport 1999). He differentiated between those signs that he thought create the enduring models that supply continuity for a society (formal, iconic signs) and those that offer the context-related connections put to use in order to make society dynamic (spatially related indexical signs). In the end, however, his model turns out to be very close to that of the Maring culture he studied, building on and thus limited by its specific linguistic ideology (Robbins 2001). The efficacy of ritual is inseparable from the efficacy of signs, and only a very finely tuned semiotic model can avoid recycling specific linguistic ideologies as theory and can account for the multifunctionality of signs and their contested interpretations.

The approach taken in this study addresses these problems directly by outlining a robust semiotic approach which necessitates a review of the theoretical

---

2 Specifically, "[I]t is probably unwise to treat the body-part nouns in expressions of internal state as inherently metaphorical. These body-part nouns simply code the locative meaning that is an essential component of all statements involving an experiencer" (Johnson 2017, 79–80).

3 For clarification of what Whorf said, as opposed to ideas attributed to him, see Lucy (1992).

assumptions. This study builds upon Silverstein's linguistic ideology as incorporated into a broader concept of "semiotic ideology" (Keane 2018). Semiotics refers to signs, non-verbal as well as verbal. In order to understand how all types of signs are employed in religious settings, this study works simultaneously in two directions: first, it examines ancient, and in the last chapter, modern, ideas about the uses of words and nonverbal signs; and second, it maps how these ideas reappear in contemporary analysis of religion. These ancient Near Eastern, Jewish, Christian, and Greco-Roman examples present language as able to do more than just refer to objects. Explicit debates about sign functions, for example, articulate which words and objects were thought to either be able, or be proper, to stand for deities and what types should not (idolatry). The ancient ideas cast long shadows and continue to shape modern analysis of ritual, religion, and culture. Looking very carefully at the modern reuse of these ideas demonstrates how they both support and limit the study of religion.

This study does not offer anything near to a complete history of the selected ancient evidence. It does not, for example, claim to offer more than a small sample of ideas about the divine name in Jewish texts. Every reader will be able to think of a string of additional examples. Each ancient example is chosen because it illustrates a particular and intriguing idea about a sign or because the ancient idea weighs heavily in recent theorizing.

The approach here is semiotic, the study of signs. As the study itself makes clear, the methods for studying sign meaning are far from monochromatic. This study is built on a very specific approach, and one purpose of this introduction is to clarify this approach. Semiotics here is dependent on the wealth of studies produced by Charles S. Peirce. The sheer breadth and constant revision of his thought has resulted in vastly different appropriations of his research.[4] The particular adaptation of Peirce mined in this study begins with Roman Jakobson's fruitful reworking of Peircean linguistics. Jakobson rethought a subset of Peirce's signs as "indexical symbols" (or "shifters") to analyze how "language self-reflexively encodes its relation to the event of speaking" (Lee 1997, 160). Silverstein (1976), building on Jakobson, distinguishes between metasemantics, the use of words to define words, and metapragmatics, the use of words for contextual implications. Linguistic functions include not only semantics (reference), and metasemantics (words about words), but also pragmatics (contextual implications) and metapragmatics (words about contextual implications).[5] While the semantic/metasemantic nexus is familiar, as for example, from the case of a dictionary

---

4 Introductions to Peirce include Lee (1997, 95–134) and Parmentier (1994, 3–22).
5 See, in addition to Silverstein (1993), Hanks (1989, 107) and Lee (1997, 166–167, 172–174).

definition (metasemantic) of a word (semantic), the pragmatic/metapragmatic functions are less familiar. Cale Johnson (2013, 27) offers a concise formulation of metapragmatic function:

> In an event of metapragmatic semiosis, the object (language) consists of a snippet of language in use and the metalinguistic comment describes the degree to which this use of language is effective, felicitous, powerful and so forth, rather than describing its semantic value.

Silverstein's theory of the multi-functionality of language offers a very different approach to issues of "performativity." The contextual implications of sign use, and especially of some words that appear to "do things," has become a major preoccupation but only in a very narrowly conceived version of such debates. Scholars of religion, recognizing that liturgical formulas are not primarily referential (propositional), readily adopted John Austin's theory of performatives (1962).[6] "Performativity" seemed to more precisely characterize the role of linguistic forms that S. J. Tambiah, for example, might have called the "magical" aspects of words. Austin, aware of additional contextual requirements for performatives to work, added a series of modifications distinguishing, for example, only some verbs as having "illocutionary" (intentional) force. The full scope of the multifunctionality of language, however, cannot be explained fully by either Austin's focus on first-person verbs or S. J. Tambiah's general description of the "magical" power of words.[7] The theory of performativity, Richard Bauman and Charles Briggs explain, "has rested on a 'literal force hypothesis' that posits a one-to-one correlation between performative utterances and illocutionary forces, even if most theorists admit that surface forms frequently do not directly signal illocutionary force" (1990, 62).

The same is true of all the speech-act theories that derive from Austin's work, including John Searle's (1969); the theories are themselves evidence of the partly opaque nature of how words "do things." As Michelle Rosaldo explained, Searle's analysis is "an ethnography—however partial—of contemporary views of human personhood and action as these are linked to culturally particular modes of speaking" (1982, 228).[8] Numerous other linguistic forms can encode Austin's "illocutionary" force, even turn-taking (Bauman and Briggs 1990, 62).

---

6 For an early example, see Wheelock (1982).

7 For an extended discussion and critique of Austin's performativity, see Lee (1997). Tambiah's groundbreaking analysis is still widely cited (Tambiah 1979). See Elizabeth Mertz (2007) on the development of semiotic anthropology.

8 See also Silverstein (1997, 269).

We can find out how effective speech and acts are conceptualized and enacted only by casting a net both much broader and finer than Austin envisioned. Therefore the present study places Austin's "performativity" within the broader semiotic conceptions of the multifunctionality of signs forged by Roman Jakobson (1960) and Michael Silverstein (1993).[9] Jakobson analyzed the relationship between language structures and language function on a much broader basis than Austin, including how language is self-reflexive and contextually linked (indexical).[10] These linkages mean that language is "performative" in all sorts of ways as linguistic forms work in two directions, simultaneously taking something about the context for granted even as they produce some aspect of that context.[11] Words, and other signs, have both presupposing and creative relations with their contexts of use. Indexical (spatial-temporal linking) understandings of signs are especially important in religion and yet likely to be lost as the historical setting changes. As Silverstein explains, "We must understand that performativity is what we have come to term indexical entailment in context: that is, we recognize that the occurrence of some organization of signs-in-context points not only to a context upon which they presume for their appropriateness (indexical presupposition), but a context that comes into being in-and-by their occurrence" (Silverstein 2016, 8).

In other words, the notion of "performativity" is a way of trying to capture the creative capacity of signs, and it needs to be understood as part of a general theory of signs. Every effective use of language and signs is dependent on socially constructed rules of use. These ideologies are what Austin was trying to capture when he added all sorts of modifiers to his basic notion of performative (illocutionary, perlocutionary, etc.). "The illocutionary force and perlocutionary effects of courtroom testimony," as Bauman and Briggs explain, "are highly dependent, for example, on evidentiary rules and broader semiotic frames that specify admissible types of relations to other bodies of written and oral discourse" (1990, 64).

Religious texts simultaneously raise metasemantic concerns of reference and definitions even as they make metapragmatic comments that capture or dispute the potential efficacy of signs. The two central points for putting these ideas to work in analyzing religious data are as follows: first, explicit metapragmatics are

---

9 In addition, see Lee (1997, 164–165, 174–177). For a model using Silverstein to rework Austin, see Sanders's study of performative utterances in Ugaritic (2004).

10 "The two dimensions of referentiality/nonreferentiality and presupposing/creative interact to specify the semiotic value of any indexical sign" (Lee 1997, 165). For additional discussions of indexical see Lee (1997, 160–164) and Parmentier (1994, 126–128, 172).

11 See the extended discussion in Lee (1997, 164–179).

not the be-all and end-all of efficacy (some aspects being beyond the user's ken); and second, metalevel comments attempt to regiment—that is, organize—a fluid process of constant interpretation of sign meaning. Scholars tend to view interpretations as being much more stable than they are. Signs do not come with premade classifications (Parmentier 2009).[12] Interpretations of sign meaning are the product of *processes* of interpretation; sign meanings are set based on guesses and claims.

As a short review of the specific Peircean sign types, sign meaning is shaped by the relation between the sign vehicle, the sign's object, and the interpretant.[13] The specific relationship of these three aspects of a sign establishes how cultural claims about similarity are constructed (X stands for Y *because it is like it in terms of Z*). The character of the sign includes three possible types: abstract possibilities (e. g., the feeling of redness), called qualisigns; actual existent signs (something red), called sinsigns; and signs marked by conventionality (conventional use of red to stand for something), called legisigns. The sign's relation to its object (its ground) includes a formal relation (icon), a relation of contiguity (index), or an arbitrary relationship (symbol). Finally, signs are also interpreted as to how they are represented by their interpretant, varying as to their degree of reality as rheme (firstness), dicent (secondness), or argument (thirdness).[14]

The most intense debates are likely to occur between very similar interpretations about, for example, how signs represent divinity. Cultural conflicts often erupt around what type of standing-for relation the sign vehicle has with the sign object (the ground). Does the sign vehicle have the same *form* as the object it represents, or does it *point to* the object it represents? The fulcrum often is how the interpretant establishes some type of similarity between the sign vehicle and the object.

Recent studies clarify the competing inclinations to interpret signs as having more formal or more contextual groundings. Interpreting as icons signs that may be seen as indexes is called rhematization, whereas interpreting as indexes what may be seen as icons is called dicentization (Keane 2018, 75). Looking first at rhe-

---

12 As Richard Parmentier states, "The assignment of a Representamen (that is, the sign vehicle) to a sign class is a positional evaluation relevant at a slice of time and from particular point of view. At each moment in the chain of semiosis a sign becomes the object of the next interpreting sign, which ideally will make the sign's reference less 'indefinite'" (2009, 141).

13 For an explanation and examples of the ten possible types of signs, see Parmentier (1994, 3–22).

14 "Whereas icon, index, and symbol classify the relationship between sign vehicle and object, rheme, dicent, and argument are metalevel construals of that relationship as represented by the interpretant" (Keane 2018, 12).

matization, Parmentier offers a clear example from a study of fifteenth-century Italian painting (1994, 19).[15] A culturally informed viewer from that period would recognize the use of expensive pigment as a sign pointing to the painting's rich patron (indexical dicent).[16] When that context is lost, the same blue pigment is interpreted via rhematization as an icon, a formal resemblance of something blue (iconic rhematic sinsign).

In the second process, dicentization, a sign that could be understood as a likeness or conventional relation is interpreted instead as a sign of an actual relation of connection (Ball 2014, 152).[17] Christopher Ball (2014) contrasts the Homeric understanding of anger as a replication of an iconic form of anger with a Freudian indexical reading of the same sign. Anger in Homer looks formally similar to anger in other Greek texts, described in the same, easily recognizable way.[18] For Freud, the anger points to past events where that anger was first felt and from whence the anger is transferred. Dicentization explains the capacity of rituals to bring participants into "actual contiguity" with social cosmologies. A sign that can be interpreted as an architectural order—in Peircean terms a rhematic iconic legisign—of the heavenly world is interpreted as placing the speaker into the heavenly world: dicent indexical legisign (Ball 2014, 160).

Theorizing Ritual

Ritual is a problem some want to solve by replacing the term "ritual" entirely (Replacers) and others by reforming it (Reformers). The problem of efficacy haunts both groups. On the side of the Replacers, the volume *Critical Terms for Religious Studies* has no entry "Ritual" but includes "Performance" (Taylor 1998). The author, Catherine Bell, outlined the advantages of this rubric: "Performance approaches seek to explore how activities create culture, authority, transcendence, and whatever forms of holistic ordering are required for people to act in meaningful and effective ways" (Bell 1998, 208). The once-standard concept of ritual, so the argument goes, is inextricably tied to connotations of rote behavior

---

15 As Gal explains, "The concept of rhematization captures the way registers that are taken up as indexes of social personae from one ideological perspective can also be construed as icons, or can be construed as icons in another ideological frame" (2013, 34).

16 As Ball explains, an index(-ical dicent sinsign) (2014, 155).

17 Thus an African object that had a specific use can be reinterpreted as a piece of art if taken as a dicent (Ball 2014). See also Keane (2018, 74).

18 The Greek reader may have had an indexical interpretation, as for example in a setting where Homer was considered a divine author.

and ossified action. It is inextricable from Protestant attacks on Catholicism. Recast as performance, rituals take their place among those social actions "by which culture is constantly constructed and reproduced" (Bell 1998, 208).

This move kicks the efficacy can down the road. It fails to note that early performance studies turned to the term "ritual," presuming that it encoded more powerful theories of social efficacy than were available in the theater arts setting of performance. At that point, ritual was regarded as the more cogent category, with greater explanations of social efficacy. As Laurel Kendall (1996, 18) notes,

In the 1960s and 1970s, avant-garde theater attempted to re-enchant performance by dipping into ethnography. The actor's experience was described as analogous to possession rituals and shamanistic journeys which evoke imagined truths in the experienced immediacy of performance, thereby making them 'real.'

As one example, Richard Schechner's groundbreaking performance schema placed ritual into a schema with play, drama, and theater (Schechner, 1988). In this schema, ritual occupies the efficacious end of the spectrum, since the participants undergo some type of transformation. Performance gains social power to the extent that it is said to resemble and function like ritual. Schechner, however, does not explain the transformative capacity of rituals beyond general comments about their dependence on "a stable order" (Schechner 1988, 134).[19]

For Schechner, ritual primarily fulfills a psychological function.[20] The war dance is a substitute for warfare. Such psychological explanations overlook some of the more disturbing aspects of rituals. Engaging in ritual warfare may lessen social sanctions against aggression. Participants may be driven toward more aggressive behavior. A war dance might lead to war. Despite these concerns, many theories of performance retain this emphasis on psychology as the ultimate explanation for efficacy in rituals.[21]

Some Replacers who reject the term "ritual," such as Talal Asad, turn instead to "habitus." This term emphasizes practices as being in and of themselves, with no eye on results or outcomes (Asad 1993). Asad avoids overly simplistic theories of ritual "magic" by having no efficacious roles for rites at all.[22] This mode of argumentation is extremely popular currently. The idea of habitus, made popular

---

19 Schechner's vague notion of ritual is repeated in other theories of performance, as noted by Kendall (1996).

20 Bell describes Schechner's theory as "a distinctive type of psychological transformation" (Bell 1998, 208).

21 Schechner is aware of this problem in other studies, as he criticizes Turner's overly adaptive psychological theories (Schechner 1988, 77).

22 His argument is very similar to J. Z. Smith's symbolic theory, discussed below. On Asad's readiness to jettison efficacy, see Hollywood (2002, 100).

by Bourdieu, posits that "rites are practices that end in themselves" (Bourdieu 1990, 18).[23] So too for Wittgenstein nothing further is achieved by kissing a picture of a loved one than the act itself (Quack 2010, 180). For noninstrumentalist Reformers and Replacers, any talk of efficacy is misplaced, since rituals have no efficacy and instead constitute behavior in and of itself, without any worldly consequences. Scientific thought relies on notions of cause and effect, whereas religious thought does not. According to this view, ritual is a purely symbolic activity whose practitioners do not expect a particular outcome from their rituals. Instead they are participating in a symbolic expression of cultural concepts.[24]

For Jonathan Z. Smith, a Reformer who offers one of the most elegant articulations of a symbolic theory, ritual is a meditation on the limitations of being human and not an attempt to assert human influence.[25] Any understanding of ritual that stresses cause and effect, Smith argues, ultimately depicts the practitioners as naïve or deluded. Anthropologists, who recorded so much of the material used in theories of ritual and magic, mistakenly took at face value the fantastic descriptions of ritual efficacy articulated by natives; scholars do not need to incorporate claims about ritual efficacy that the natives themselves do not believe.

Smith's theory of ritual is constructed to avoid anything that smacks of James George Frazer's Victorian-era theory of magic (Frazer 1947). Frazer's primitives employed rituals doomed to failure, their actions based on mistaken uses of analogical thinking (sympathy, contagion).[26] Smith counterargued that natives are aware of the limitations of human action and meditate on these limitations via their rituals. Any attempt to posit a simple connection between, for example, a perfectly controlled hunt ritual and an actual chaotic hunt would be a mistake, since the operating principles are so very different (Quack 2010).

The severed connection between ritual and daily life outlined by Smith assigns to rituals a powerful but strictly delineated role. For Smith, rituals demonstrate to participants what the world would be like if everyone could act like a god instead of having to observe the limitations of being human. Smith's claim is that religious ritual, like obsessional behavior, is symbolic and does

---

23 Bourdieu draws on Mauss but changes the emphasis considerably, as noted by Quack (2010, 77).

24 For classic and still influential versions of this position, see Quack (2010, 170–181) and Winch (1964).

25 In Burton Mack's (1987, 48) elucidation, "Religion does not change anything at all; rather, it is a way of coping, creatively, with the contingent."

26 For Frazer's two basic laws of magic ("like produces like," and "once connected, always connected"), see Frazer (1947, 11–13).

not change or affect anything. Smith cites Freud's emphasis on the ceremonial as "an exaggeration of an ordinary and justifiable orderliness" and compares it with Lévi-Strauss's notion of ritual as parceling out and repetition (J. Z. Smith 1987a, 111). The draw of a symbolic theory is its stance against overly simplistic notions of efficacy as, for example, presented by the credulous anthropologists Smith critiqued. Giving up on the quest for a theory of efficacy, the reasoning goes, is better than using an outdated theory that makes the natives look foolish.

The motivation shared by some Reformers and some Replacers for this type of theory is laudable, since it frees the practitioners from believing in what appear to be ridiculously simple or misguided notions of cause and effect. Indeed, as Penner noted, "one of the strengths of the symbolic approach is its criticism of ethnocentric explanations of religious beliefs and practices" (Penner 1989, 71). The caricatured voodoo-doll model of ritual has been left behind, as have outdated theories of primitive magic.

However, an act-in-itself approach to ritual is fraught with problems.[27] It seems difficult to believe that the modes of thought represented in rituals possess this complete differentiation from issues of cause and effect (Penner 1989, 70–71). A symbolic approach cannot explain the full range of roles that rituals fill in society. As Richard Parmentier reminds us, "ritual in many cultural traditions functions to change social relationships, convey divine powers, cure diseases, or coerce natural forces" (1994, 128). For social constructivists, ritual is the engine of social construction.

Symbolic explanations negate the statements by participants who believe that their rituals are supposed to have specific effects and thus make the participants look ridiculous. The implicit accusation that participants are wrong in their understanding of rituals is not itself grounds for rejecting symbolic theories, but negating their direct statements about rituals is an odd way to develop more indigenous-friendly interpretations. The theorist may be rescuing the indigenous people from accusations of misguided action, but he is also telling them that they do not understand their actions. In sum, symbolic theories may look less pejorative on the surface, but they are not. They fail to offer a theoretical basis for the analysis of symbols. Furthermore, symbolic theories cannot account for the perceived efficacy of rituals, and they eviscerate ritual of any real purpose.[28]

---

27 See the criticisms by Penner (1989, 69–72).

28 On the issue of perceived efficacy, see the important comments in Parmentier (1994, 47–69), especially on page 69.

At the level of semiotics, a symbolic approach does not tell us what the rituals are symbolic of or how to decode the symbols. Clifford Geertz, for example, placed symbols at the heart of his definition of religion but did not tell us how they work. The notion of symbol is used by Geertz "sometimes as an aspect of reality, sometimes of its representation" (Asad 1993, 30).[29] If ritual symbols are about representation, a theory of sign representation is vital.

The power of rituals is very limited in recent scholarship. In Seligman and Weller's (2012) study, ritual is limited to the "as-if" of play, as when a child pretends that a toy airplane can fly.[30] Play helps both mother and child adjust to an external reality that is not affected by their actions. The line between the fantasy world of play, which includes ritual and performativity, and the hard-knocks world of reality is clearly drawn. This is a stunning limitation for ritual.[31]

Ritual, in the symbolic approach, is a philosophical endeavor that helps people realize they have little power. Ritual "recognizes the ambiguous nature of reality and registers it, rather than denying it" (Seligman and Weller 2012, 96). This is a much less effective concept of ritual as creating aspects of the harsh reality of social existence. Ritual can help a president deal with the conflicts inherent in being both president and a father. But Seligman and Weller's model cannot explain the rituals that made him a president and articulate a specific role as a father. It cannot explain why, for example, Obama had to take the oath of office twice because of a ritual slip-up or how American rites shape the role of the father.[32]

Seligman and Weller (Seligman et al. 2008) limit the psychological efficacy of ritual posited by other psychologists.[33] Erik Erikson, for example, argued that ritual can overcome ambivalence (1966). In the version offered by Seligman and Weller (Seligman et al. 2008) ritual *preserves* ambivalence. Being able to hold on to ambivalence, they posit, is a more complex mental state than using the defense mechanisms of outright denial or splitting.[34] Ambivalence is a mature psychological state. If rituals, however, only preserve ambivalence, they can never lead to any working-through and psychological resolution.

---

29 Asad contrasts Geertz's ill-defined use of symbol with Peirce's system (Asad 1993, 30n30).
30 This limitation is similar to the "as-if" quality commonly associated with theater, once again building in a weak-efficacy theory.
31 And, it would seem, for psychoanalysis as well, despite the fact that one of the authors is a psychoanalyst.
32 CNN (2009). For wedding rituals creating American family roles, see Auslander (2013).
33 Winnicott is discussed below in Chapter Six, pages 121 f.
34 For these defenses, see Laplanche and Pontalis (1973, 109 – 111).

Outline of Chapters

Chapter One, "Ancient Ideologies of Ineffability and Their Echoes," traces ideologies of language as a guide to truth, even as that truth is defined by the *limits* of language. The linguistic theories of some ancient exegetes started with the basic concept that words are names for objects. These names, however, were not capable of fully defining "hard to describe" (*arrhētos*) divinity. Despite this limitation, names remained the best formal representations of divinity and thus were central to both philosophical investigation and ritual practices. The two "fashions of speaking" about divine truth coexisted in a delicate balance: first, that names describe divinity; and second, that names fail to completely describe divinity, which is in some sense "ineffable." When philosophers choose to emphasize the former view, divine names are interpreted as formal representations of divinity. In the case of the gap between name and object, a type of "reverse definition" (a god is not just "good") highlighted the inability to fix divine names semantically, casting divinity just beyond the limits of discourse.

In the work of scholars such as Michael Sells (1994), the modern ineffable shifts focus from divinity to the Self (the locus of modern truth), which is by definition both hidden and real. Based on this notion of the "hard to describe" but true self, religious experiences are by definition supposed to represent truth in the same way that the ancient names revealed and concealed a truth about the deity. Modern scholars have taken these different tropes out of their rhetorical contexts and elevated them to the level of theory. The ineffable is now a hidden self, and linguistic structure proves the truth of a mystical experience.

Chapter Two compares two linguistic ideologies, Austin's speech acts and Althusser's naming ideology. In *Excitable Speech*, Judith Butler compares these two models for the social efficacy of language (Butler 1997a). Of the two, she prefers Austin's theory, arguing that Althusser's is rarely used in general society. Showing that it is far from rare, this chapter turns to a series of examples from the history of Israelite and Jewish divine-name ideologies. Divine naming ideologies, unlike the more recent speech-act model, have been used extensively over diverse historical periods and relate the contextual implications of words to other modalities (other types of signs, such as statues). While neither ideology is sufficient for a theoretical model of the multifunctionality of language, divine naming ideologies point to cross-culturally valid similarities in the functionality of names.

Chapter Three focuses on debates about proper and improper representations of the deity by both verbal and non-verbal signs. These debates are never a reliable description of actual practice. The once-standard view of Israelite religious practices as anti-iconic has undergone a revolution. After reviewing this revolution in brief, the chapter turns to several striking examples of sign use in cultic settings. These contrast sharply with the anti-iconic vision of cult Josephus presents; he argues that Jewish beliefs are superior based on values shared with the larger society. He entered into debates about the role of images eagerly, since it was an opportunity to offer a commercial, as it were, for Jewish cultic practices. The final section of the chapter builds upon the classic study of idolatry by Halbertal and Margalit, arguing that it constructs an abstract theory of idolatry that is, once again, the elevation of a historically contingent argument about proper images to the level of abstract theory (Halbertal and Margalit 1992).

Chapter Four examines a Late Antique linguistic ideology that Paul made famous when he differentiated between the *gramma* (written letter) and the *pneuma* (spirit). "Spirit," in Paul's usage, refers to something highly valued, something that points toward a person's internal motivations and hence is inherently meaningful. The exact reference is less important than the positive evaluation of the term. "Letter," in contrast with spirit, has a limited linguistic role. With this strategy, a distorting hierarchy is built between a linguistic unit that has less meaning and no allegorical implications (letter) and one that opens up an endless chain of related metaphorical implications (spirit). Many modern scholars have recycled the spirit/letter model for not just theological but also general historical purposes, as some examples will demonstrate. In contrast, Mira Balberg (2017), in her insightful analysis of rabbinic discourse about sacrifice, attempts to replace a limiting "letter"/"spirit"-based model of sacrifice. The rabbis, she argues, envisage sacrifice as a set of actions carried out even after the destruction of the Temple. For them sacrifice is a reality and not a metaphor. Balberg has opened up but not resolved the question of how to compare distinct sign representations of sacrifice, a question that can be further probed with a more robust semiotic analysis.

Chapter Five focuses on two Jewish ascent liturgies, one from Qumran and the other from a hard-to-date non-standard rabbinic text. Both examples offer distinct challenges to modern readers since the texts appear to have the striking ritual efficacy of transporting a human into the heavenly world. A Peircean mode of analysis reveals that dicentization works in the first text by transposing the human priestly realm into the divine realm, transforming the human priests and their liturgical recitation into part of the angelic cult. In the second, the chain of rabbinic transmission recounted in the (re)telling of an ascent elevates the reciter into the heavenly world via both iconic (mapping) and indexical (context-related) signs. In this case, the model of ritual efficacy is based on the rabbinic linguistic ideology—that is, that angelic liturgy fueled by divine names.

Chapter Six investigates the Burning Man festival, which, like many contemporary rituals, is characterized by both participants and scholars as an example of "spirituality." This term represents an attempt by participants to distance themselves from institutions they distrust. From a Peircean viewpoint, Burning Man is centered on signs that gain meaning only through interpretation, reflecting modern theories of art interpretation. The polysemy at Burning Man offers semiotic ideologies in which regimented meanings, while influenced by community principles, are dependent on personal interpretation.

1 Ancient Ideologies of Ineffability and Their Reverberations

The Platonic Legacy about Words

Ancient theological debates echo with the question: What can and cannot be expressed in language? Some ancient philosophers argued that it was impossible to describe a deity in words. The task was as hopeless as capturing a deity in stone. Yet perhaps words are the best tools available for investigating the nature of divinity. They should be exploited as much as possible provided that their limits are recognized.

In the late second century CE, the Christian exegete Basilides (fl. 120–140 CE), in his writings on ethics and cosmology, posited that the deity is beyond naming.[1] Engaging in a debate with contemporary philosophical (mainly Platonic) discourse, Basilides emphasized that the deity is ineffable. The term that Basilides used was *arrhēton,* an adjective formed from the α-privative combined with "to say/speak," often translated "ineffable." The term had several meanings in ancient Greek, including: "unspoken" (*Odyssey* 14.466), "what should not be spoken" (Herodotus, *Hist.* 5.83), and "something horrible to utter" (Sophocles, *Elektra* 203). Basilides's use is closest to Plato's, "what cannot be spoken" (*Sophist* 238c). John Whittaker describes the use of the term *arrhēton* as commonplace in Middle Platonic speculation.[2]

Although Basilides did not invent these ideas, he crystallized a new version of Platonic ineffability, one that conflates ideas about words and matter with an increasingly monotheistic theology. Basilides's particular theology of ineffability

---

1 Basilides's writings are known only from citations preserved by other ancient writers mostly hostile to him. Fragments of Basilides appear in Irenaeus, *Against Heresies* 1.24.3–7; Hippolytus, *Refutation of All Heresies* 7.8–15, 10.10; and Clement of Alexandria, *Strom.* 7. For translations of and commentaries on the fragments see Layton (1987). For discussions, see Layton (1989), May (1994, 62–84), and Pearson (2007, 132–144). Layton (1989, 138–139) considers the citations from Clement and Irenaeus genuine; May (1994, 62–84) prefers the citations from Hippolytus. Resolving this issue is beyond the scope of this chapter. Most of the Basilides citations discussed in this chapter are from Hippolytus. Layton (1989) wisely sets aside the label "gnostic" given to Basilides by his opponents. On the problematic nature of the use of "gnostics/Gnosticism," see M. Williams (1996).
2 Whittaker also cites the Pythagorean Lysis (1969, 368). Clement claims God is ineffable (*Strom.* 5.65.2) as part of his extensive use of the α-privative, even as he claims that divine names can be indicative of the deity's power (*Strom.* 5.82.1–2). For further discussion, see Hägg (2006).

https://doi.org/10.1515/9783110768602-002

build upon contemporaneous writers who used the term *arrhēton* as an adjective to describe the deity. He interpreted the common use of the term as simply one more in a string of attempts to name the deity, this time with the name "Ineffable."[3] These writers, he claimed, failed to note that they were simply substituting a new name for the ones they considered inappropriate; they missed the central point: that the deity cannot be named at all.

As an exegete, Basilides found a textual basis for his claim in Ephesians 1:20 – 21, which states, "God enacted this in Christ when he raised him from the dead and seated him at his right hand in the heavenly places, far above all rule and authority and power and dominion, and above every name that is named" (my translation). The verse stresses the elevation of Christ, juxtaposing name with a variety of terms for sovereignty. Basilides turned the phrase into a metaphysical statement about divinity, placing divinity beyond naming in accordance with a particular linguistic ideology about the function of naming. As Basilides explains it, "What is named is not absolutely ineffable [Gk. *arrhēton*], since we call one thing ineffable and another not even ineffable. For what is not even ineffable is not named ineffable but is above every name that is named" (Hippolytus, *Haer.* 7.20.8). Basilides insisted on rejecting all names in order to move the deity to yet another level of transcendent mystery, one step beyond the direct reference of names. He is showing off, doing some one-upmanship in "an attempt to achieve the ultimate in negative theology" (Whittaker 1969, 368).

This metaphysical stance reworks ancient ideas about names. In early Greek traditions, as in numerous texts that became part of Hebrew Scriptures, it was valid and necessary to distinguish between many different gods with different names. These names were sometimes proper names (Zeus, Yahweh, etc.) but took many forms. The ancient fashion of naming permitted easily turning a noun or an adjective into the name of a deity. Nouns and names were not distinguished as different linguistic entities, so "All-Powerful" could successfully be used as a name for a deity.

Basilides's concerns about names and the limits of language were shared by contemporaries who preserved and adjusted ideas from Plato. In sum, Basilides's linguistic ideology constituted an extension of general ideas about words found in Plato's *Cratylus* and in later interpretations of this text (Whittaker 1969, 370). Although interpretations varied in the ancient world, a few central fault lines of interpretation emerged. In the *Cratylus*, Socrates rejects Hermoge-

---

3 Jufresa argues Basilides is countering, in particular, the rabbinic ideology of a powerful and not-to-be-spoken divine Name (1981, 1), but the context for his comments is much broader.

nes's conventional theory of naming. He is also concerned with Cratylus's support of a single natural name for each object. Although debates continue about what Socrates is ultimately arguing, Socrates never appears to accept the idea that names are entirely conventional (Sedley 2003, 148). As Rachel Barney explains, "Once conventionalism is defeated, conservatism can no longer be assumed, and the way is clear for the critical, revisionist—not to mention madly counterintuitive—account of 'natural correctness' which Socrates proceeds to deliver" (1997, 158).

Names offer the best descriptor of divinity, since they have a natural and nonconventional relationship with what they stand for. A name imitates the thing's being (Sedley 2003, 83).[4] According to the *Cratylus*, "A thing's name is its verbal portrait, in the sense that it is by virtue not just of its having been assigned to that thing but also of its mimetic description of it that the word secures its status as that thing's name" (Sedley 2003, 149). This interpretive stance depends on two distinct ideas; first, a specific notion of a name giver, and second, the notion of names as tools.[5] According to the first premise, the individuals who gave names to objects encoded descriptions of those object in the names (*Crat.* 391b–427d). Names are "telescoped descriptions of their *nominata*" (Sedley 2003, 36). In Imogen Smith's terms, "names are non-arbitrary since their internal constitutions render them 'correct for' the objects they name" (2014, 77).[6]

According to the second idea, names are a special kind of tool (*Crat.* 386d–390e). Smith argues that the tool analogy supports the idea that names are not arbitrary, since "The tool analogy ... advances a radical linguistic naturalism which follows from the conjunction of certain key claims" (2014, 95). Just as tool makers require a special expertise, so too do name makers.[7] Names (and nouns) are the best formal representations of divinity and are therefore central to both philosophical investigation and ritual practices.[8]

---

4 A more serious Socratic dismissal of natural theories is argued for by, among others, B. Williams (1982).

5 This argument, Imogen Smith contends, "comprises a largely deductive argument making appeal to the Forms and proceeds from a rejection of a traditional Platonic concern, Protagorean relativism" (2014, 77).

6 See also Barney's (1997, 160) description of the Platonic expert knowledge that is required to decide if the name-giver knew what he was doing.

7 Smith points specifically to "Socrates' introduction of Species-Forms (389b8), which finely circumscribe the features of the specific tools that instantiate them," with a distinction between the crafts of names' expert maker and their expert user (2014, 78).

8 The preserved fragments of Basilides are primarily exegetical, but there is no doubt that he employed divine names in rites, as other early Christians did.

No distinction is made between names and nouns. Barney explains, "In keeping with standard Greek usage, 'name', *onoma*, is used in the *Cratylus* for common nouns as well as proper names; at various points we also find adjectives (412c2, e1), verbs in the infinitive form (414a8–b1) and participles (421c5–6) described as names" (1997, 143). Since names are not distinguished from other linguistic units, the same investigations can be made of nouns and even adjectives. Defining all these linguistic units was an important tool for investigating reality. Etymology, another such tool, works on linguistic units from names and nouns to adjectives (Sedley 2003, 4). The same subject-plus-predication truth that can be uncovered by means of dialogic investigation is located, writ small, in every name.

In short, in the *Cratylus* two "fashions of speaking" coexist in a delicate balance: names best represent divinity, and at the same time names fail to completely represent divinity. Names by definition have their limitations (Sedley 2003, 5).[9] The natural, or "ideal" names of the Forms, for example, are elusive (Kretzmann 1971). Truth must be pursued at the level of names but also beyond the level of names. For example, dialogue itself is a form of linguistic investigation. Dialogues are central, because Plato thought that conversation is the structure of thought itself (Sedley 2003, 1). The form of a dialogue is the most extended Socratic investigation into words' meanings and their implications and thus into truth (Nehamas 1992, 179).[10]

When Basilides was writing, the representational capacity of material language was also being rethought just as the deity was increasingly seen as having a role other than that of matter organizer. Basilides was one of the first Christian exegetes to explicitly claim the deity did not make any use of preexistent matter in creating the world. As with the names of gods, here too Basilides pushes the exegetical envelope. While a full description of this process is beyond the scope of this chapter, a quick review of the contours of antimaterial sentiments helps us understand his strategy.

---

9 A nonverbal technique might be the use of silence which is attributed to Socrates. On the difficulty of attributing a specific meaning to his silence, see Nehamas (1992).

10 Alex Long (2008) argues that Plato exhibits a very broad notion of dialogue, varying from example to example, even including the soul dialogue with the self as in the *Sophist*.

The Antimaterialist Tipping Point: Representation beyond Name and Matter

Basilides offered one of the first statements of the doctrine known as "creation from nothing."[11] Based on Jewish and Christian polemics, most modern readers assume that the Hebrew Scriptures depict an all-powerful deity who creates the world out of nothing.[12] However, imagery preserved in Genesis, Psalms, and prophetic writings conceives of creation as ordering chaos rather than as making matter out of nothing.[13] While Greek Creation stories included a range of options about creation and matter, the craftsman deity from Plato and Aristotle works with some type of formless matter—a philosophical version of the narrative imagery of primordial matter found in numerous biblical Creation myths.[14] Belief in preexistent matter is not only clearly presupposed in various ancient Hebrew texts but also was slow to change, which is not surprising given the conservative attitudes toward cosmologies. It took centuries to complete the slow ascent up the monotheism mountain to meet the deity who made everything out of nothing. As ancient Near Eastern religions moved into their Late Antique phase, the Chosen People's deity was refracted through a strand of internationalist rhetoric found in some prophets. By the first century CE, international trends toward monotheistic ways of describing the creator deity had begun to clash with textual depictions of the deity in the Hebrew Scriptures and in Plato's *Timaeus* as the organizer of preexistent matter.[15] The deity was imagined as being too powerful and too mighty in his omnipotence to have even the smallest shreds of primordial matter as a rival. According to this view, the deity adopted not only local but even foreign kings based on a supranationalistic protomonotheism (Bickerman and Smith 1976, 119).[16] This nationalistic stance paralleled the Greek belief, standard by the fifth century BCE, that Zeus represented a "supreme cosmic intellect" (Dillon 1999, 69). Whereas at one time a theologian won by presenting his divin-

---

11 Although he may well not have been the first to articulate this idea, his is the first extant.
12 Sedley's mention that Genesis is usually understood to assume that God created the world out of nothing is evidence of the staying power of that idea (2007, xvii).
13 See Gen 1:1–2; Isa 44:24, 45:18, 51:10; Jer 5:22; Prov 8:22–31; Ps 74:12–17, 89:1–14, 104; and Job 26:7–14; discussed by Levenson (1994, 3–13).
14 See for example, Plato, *Timaeus* 50d, and Aristotle, *Physics* 191a10. Another model of creation in both ancient Near Eastern and Greek texts was genealogical. Anaxagoras's Mind is closer to a nature-based model of a farmer with seeds than to an omnipotent creator; atomists want nature to work by itself (Sedley 2007, 25).
15 "That even a divine creator would, like any craftsman, have to use preexisting materials is an assumption that the ancient Greeks apparently never questioned" (Sedley 2007, xvii).
16 Evident, for example, in Isaiah 40–54.

ity as greater than someone else's, now he attained the winning edge by elevating the deity right out of the realm of materiality.

For both Platonists and biblical exegetes, the doctrine of *creatio ex nihilo* emerged in a series of partial steps as matter was increasingly subordinated to its creator. Plato presented his Creation story in the *Timaeus* as a myth, which "leaves the reader a good deal of room for varying degrees of deliteralization" (Sedley 2007, 100). Crantor (335–275 BCE), for example, argued that Plato implied by the term "created" that the "world is dependent on a cause other than itself".[17] Aristotle claimed that followers of Plato employed the phrasing "what does not have being" for matter (*Phys.* 1.192a6–8). David Winston characterizes this as implying nonexistent in an incidental sense, only one of several ways of being nonexistent (1971, 186).[18]

Strikingly similar partial steps are found in Jewish exegetical circles, another important context for Basilides.[19] Philo (25 BCE–50 CE), a Jewish exegete who wrote extensively on the topic of Creation, presents an interesting comparison; he advocated for a more ambiguous version of creation from nothing while also retaining a greater role for divine naming.[20] In line with fellow Platonists, Philo "removed the Creator-God to a superior transcendence," but he did so unevenly (Blowers 2012, 53). Philo only ambiguously embraced what Winston calls a "double-Creation theory," creation of matter and then of the world (1971,

---

17 Preserved in Proclus, *In Tim.* 1.277.8. See Dillon (1977, 42).

18 A very similar claim is attributed to another of Plato's disciples, Hermodorus. See Simplicius, *In Phys.* 1.9 (May 1994, 17), and also Diogenes Laertius 2.106, 3.6. Preexistent matter continued to be taken for granted in exegetical discussions up through the sixth century CE and beyond. For a survey of rabbinic interpretations of preexistent matter, see Niehoff (2006) and Winston (1971, 191). For Christian interpretations, see Blowers (2012) and May (1994).

19 The similarity is rejected by those looking for a unique Christian stance on creation. For example, Blowers's detailed study of Late Antique cosmological debates repeats early Christian claims of uniqueness, finding a "domestication" of Greco-Roman ideas first in Jewish and then in the Christian exegetes (2012). Similarly Gerhard May tries to limit the Jewish use of Platonic ideas, arguing that Hellenistic Jews did not invent the idea of *creatio ex nihilo* because they did not "engage in a fundamental debate with the Platonic and Stoic doctrine of principles" (1994, 21).

20 On Philo's creation imagery in general, see Dillon (1977, 158–161), Sorabji (1983, 203–209), and Wolfson (1948, 300–310). For additional bibliography, see May (1994, 9–22). For an attempt to make a synthetic reading of Philo's various views, see Blowers (2012, 46–66), and compare Maren Niehoff's argument (2006) that different audiences affect his mode of argumentation. Philo makes a very complex, and not entirely consistent, argument about divine names, because he believes, like a good Platonist, that they contain important information about what they name, as discussed in the next chapter.

199n140).[21] Philo states in *Confusion* (136), "God created space and place simultaneously with bodies." Given that some Platonists refer to matter by the term "space," Philo appears to be using contemporary theology, Aristotelian and Platonic.[22] Eudorus, interpreting Aristotle in the first century BCE, argued that the One created matter.[23] Matter is subordinated to the deity not via a direct statement of creation from nothing but by the more indirect claim that the deity is the cause of the essence of everything, including matter.

Basilides attempts to reformulate the craftsman role for the deity and heighten the deity's power over names simultaneously, arguing that there was a time when not even nothing existed (*Haer.* 7.20). The world has more things than can be named, and homonyms are also a problem, so it is necessary to use one's mind in a wordless manner (*Haer.* 7.20.4).[24] The world was contained in a seed that was sowed and planted by the deity. The seed is equated with the word of the deity who made the world through speech, Basilides argued, citing Psalm 32:6 in the Septuagint version, "By the word of the Lord the heavens were made, by the breath of his mouth, all their host" (*Haer.* 7.22.3).

At the moment when the word became "flesh" that is, when it was spoken in material language, the materiality of the world came into being. Thus "nonbeing" was turned into being. Basilides explains, "Just as the grain of mustard comprises all things simultaneously. ... In this way 'nonexistent' God made the world out of nonentities, casting and depositing some One seed that contained in itself a conglomeration of the germs of the world" (*Haer.* 7.21–22). The material seed the deity planted appears to be the Word, with everything then being generated from the Word. These theological shifts articulated with shifting linguistic ideologies. For Basilides, the only deity who exists did so far divorced from the world of matter and did not need any of the names found in earlier Scriptural texts.

---

21 Preexistent matter seems to be presumed in *Creation* 5.21. The now-familiar phrase "formless matter" appears in *Heir* 140 and *Spec. Laws* 1.328; the alternative phrasing "out of preexistent matter," in *Moses* 2.267 and *Spec. Laws* 2.225. *Contra*, Sorabji argues that in *On Providence* 1 and 2 the deity created the cosmos and matter simultaneously (1983, 203–209).

22 Alcinous, *Handbook on Platonism* 8; Aristotle, *Physics* 209b11. See Grant (1952, 141).

23 Alexander of Aphrodisias's third-century CE commentary on Aristotle's *Metaphysics* credits Eudorus with emending Aristotle's text in order to show that the One created matter (Dillon 1977, 128n121 and Dorrie 1944). Eudorus may have done this to support Pythagorean ideas, raising the question of whether Pythagorean doctrine was another force toward an emanation version of creation (a form of subordination of matter to the deity).

24 Unfortunately, the excerpt does not explore this idea in greater detail. See Whittaker (1992) for a brief discussion.

Basilides's status as a heretic and specifically as a gnostic in the eyes of some early Christians may explain a hesitancy by modern scholars to attribute importance to Basilides's articulation of what became a central theological doctrine.[25] The expanded creative-power doctrine itself was ultimately embraced by those who claimed to be orthodox once the new position was incorporated theologically and displaced the old. Basilides, however, was never rehabilitated.[26]

On Beyond Language: Linguistic Ideologies of Nonverbal Representation

Not too long after Basilides, the Platonic commentator Plotinus (204 – 270 CE) reformulated Platonic linguistic ideas for very specific exegetical reasons.[27] Plotinus was, like Basilides, attempting to systematize and modernize a set of contradictory writings, in this case Plato's treatises (Porphyry, *Life of Plotinus* 15). Plotinus's work was ad hoc, primarily metalinguistic interpretations that posited new definitions for Platonic and, to some extent, Aristotelian terms.[28] Plotinus shared many of Basilides's ideas about language, insisting that an even stricter ineffability was necessary for a pursuit of the truth. Although he was never able to systematize his ideas, Plotinus did present some propositions that helped domesticate the problem of potentially unwieldly matter.

According to Porphyry, Plotinus gave public discourses where he was presented with various conundrums of Platonic interpretation. He responded to questions from his students, a smattering of Roman senators (*Life* 7) and even members of the imperial court (*Life* 12).[29] His exegetical success was mixed. His treatises were found unintelligible; his discourse was described as "a great deal of wandering and futile talk" (*Life* 3), and the man himself was "despised as a word spinner" (*Life* 18). Many of his points were rejected by later exegetes.[30]

---

25 As for example by May (1994, 76n70). See also the hesitancy in Blowers (2012, 178 – 179, 182).

26 Thus the ancient impetus for subordinating primordial matter to the deity was not to fight heresy, as argued by May (1994) for the Christian material and Winston (1971, 192n12) for the Jewish.

27 There is no evidence that Plotinus had read Basilides, contra Jufresa (1981). In the vast bibliography on Plotinus, for the particular issues raised here see Ahbel-Rappe (2000), Dillon (1996, 2002), Rist (1967, 213 – 230), and Schroeder (1996).

28 Schroeder describes Plotinus's writings as "intertextual metalanguage" (2002, 34).

29 Plotinus wrote his treatises down only in his fifties and in hurried fashion (Porphyry, *Life of Plotinus* 8). Porphyry organized them and gave them their titles (*Life* 4).

30 Frederic Schroeder describes some of Plotinus's work as "impossible interpretations" (2002, 23), while Pauliina Remes notes that "Plotinus' commitment to monism seems slightly compro-

Plotinus's dense and sometimes cryptic statements are often open to more than one interpretation. Like his student Porphyry, who edited Plotinus's treatises and composed a biography, every reader has to make a personal synthesis of Plotinus's corpus.[31]

The problems with, and models for, naming were central to Plotinus's investigations. He explains in the *Enneades:* "We speak of the unspeakable; wishing to signify it as best we can, we name it" (*Enn.* 5.5.6).[32] The general themes of his linguistic ideology are familiar from Plato: language has its limits, but it is the best strategy for locating truth. Investigating names, and all words, by investigating definitions is the heart of philosophical endeavors at the same time that the limits of discourse are acknowledged. Schroeder summarizes this position as follows: "Language will never disclose the One. ... Yet we may use language about, or discuss, the One, so long as we are aware of the limitations of speech" (Schroeder 1996, 344).

Naming in this broad sense clarifies reality at several different levels simultaneously. Plotinus mentions, for example, that the Pythagoreans name their god Apollo. This name means "Not-many," which demonstrates one level of wisdom. At the same time, like Basilides and other contemporaries, Plotinus emphasized the limits of language for the highest level of divinity: "The One is in truth beyond all statement" (*Enn.* 5.3.13).[33] Using a section from Plato's *Parmenides* 137B–144E (especially 141E-142 A) as an exegetical key to the linguistic ideology, Plotinus defines the metalinguistic realm of ineffability: the One is without attributes (Bussanich 2007, 61). In short, Plotinus posits that although nouns are the best descriptors, rejecting definitions and descriptors can help overcome both the materiality of language and its predication about a god who is also mistakenly identified with materiality.

Given that his linguistic ideology is based on a very specific notion of naming as definition, it should be expected that a gap between a name and what it names will become increasingly important. Increasingly, monotheistic theology

---

mised by his descriptions of matter's nature as always the opposite of form and goodness" (2008, 95). She also notes many places where later Platonists rejected Plotinus's ideas (Remes 2008, 71). For Porphyry, Damascius, and Proclus's reworkings of the concept the One, see Dillon (1996, 122–123).

31 Sometimes his students seem unwilling to pursue an enigmatic saying, as in the case of his statement that it is for the gods to come to him.

32 On Plotinus's ideas about language, see in particular Ahbel-Rappe (2000) and Schroeder (1996). Jufresa argues that Plotinus was dependent on Basilides, but there is no evidence of direct links, nor are they necessary (1981).

33 See *Parmenides* 137B–144E, where the One is denied Being since that would imply it is not perfect (Dillon 1996, 121–122).

placed greater distance between the deity and matter, always modeled on the gap built into naming. Again like Basilides, Plotinus will engage in one-upmanship about how best to investigate the most complex limitations of naming.[34] Plotinus's proof of the superiority of his interpretations is ultimately his status as a more divine being than the other interpreters. On the ancient scale, his level of divinity had to be very high. Plotinus revealed these credentials on a few occasions, either hinting at or having someone around him clarify just how divine a being he truly was or claiming that his interpretations had brought him into contact with divinity (Porphyry, *Life* 10.14 – 33).

To supplement his divine status and his use of illuminating Platonic discourse, Plotinus outlines other modes of representation which do not suffer from the problems of names. These include sign modalities other than definition, such as Egyptian hieroglyphs, prophetic letters written in nature (*Enn.* 3.3.6), and visual images.[35] In semiotic terms, these are understood by Plotinus to be iconic (formal) representations of divinity that do not suffer from the gap found in naming. For example, he encourages his reader to imagine a diaphanous sphere.[36] Visualization is presented as a solution to the problem posed by the linguistic ideology. In this linguistic (or perhaps more correctly semiotic) ideology, the gap between name and object can be overcome when discourse is avoided. "Plotinus' problem is that he needs to convey a theory of truth that is precisely non-representational, without the unwanted result that reality collapses into mere representations" (Ahbel-Rappe 2000, 28). Internalized thought overcomes some of the problems of definition, with mental images breaking down the boundary of a self/other model of name/object. These semiotic structures lead to truth because of their formal representation of reality at a nonverbal level and their indexical capacity to make the truth co-present.

Plotinus rejects other interpreters by distorting their interpretive processes. For example, he reads astrological texts literally to distort their depiction of the future (Lawrence 2007, 28).[37] He vehemently attacks Know-It-Alls (gnostics), the ancient term of abuse applied by some Christian theologians to Basilides. He did not like their use of myths (despite Plato's use of myths) and their rituals that used symbolism, breathings, and secret divine names (*Against the Gnostics*,

---

34 For a discussion of this gap, see Ahbel-Rappe (2000, 28).

35 For the hieroglyphs, see *Enn.* 5.8.6, discussed in Ahbel-Rappe (2000, 107); for letters in nature, see Schroeder (2002, 27); for the nonpropositional status of visual images see Ahbel-Rappe (2000, 25 – 44) and Bertini (2007, 40 – 41).

36 For imagination, see Ahbel-Rappe (2000, 79 – 80).

37 Michael Williams points out that the distinction between "gnostic" and Platonic notions of fate is overdrawn (1992).

Enn. 2.9).[38] He belittles stories about a revolt by the demiurge against a female figure. He also ridicules their incantations, despite the fact that he is in favor of prayer (*Enn.* 2.9.14). The secret names offend Plotinus's sensibilities and his notions of how to investigate truth. Plotinus states,

> In the sacred formulas they inscribe, purporting to address the Supernal Beings ... they are simply uttering spells and appeasements and evocations in the idea that these Powers will obey a call and be led about by a word from any of us who is in some degree trained to use the appropriate forms in the appropriate way—certain melodies, certain sounds, specially directed breathings, sibilant cries, and all else to which is ascribed magic potency upon the Supreme. (*Enn.* 2.9.14)

These speakers use words without understanding what they are doing, thereby lapsing into magical thinking. He derides their overly simplistic linguistic ideas, subordinating the deity to the materiality of speech and the will of the speaker. Better they should engage in dialogical investigations of Platonic texts with him, investigation that would teach them the correct contours and limits of effective speech.

In sum, Plotinus's fashion of ineffability emerged as both an ontology (how divinity came into being in the first place) and an epistemology (how we can learn about divinity). Plotinus's reshaping of terms firmly moved the deity beyond any formal connection between name and thing, reformulating Basilides's rejection of names.[39] Plotinus differed from Basilides in insisting that the deity was unified, not multiple, and thus entirely beyond, and not simply above, matter (as Basilides had claimed). This emphasis set new limits to reference since it was not possible to refer to something that stood entirely outside the normal standing-for relationships of language.

A Modern Interpretation of Plotinus

Michael Sells (1994) offers an interpretation of Plotinus that has become the cornerstone of a modern theory of ineffability. Sells's apophatic ideology offers one more level of interpretation drawn from the Greek linguistic ideology of definition and naming. It is possible to find reality working through language, but

---

38 Basilides, for example, mentions the secret name "Caulacau" (Irenaeus, *Against the Heresies* 24.5, and May 1994, 63). For commonalities between Plotinus's interpretations and "gnostic" concepts, see Turner (1992).
39 Plotinus's move created as many problems as it solved. For example, he failed to develop a consistent theory of evil.

in this model reality is modeled on the *reverse* of standard notions of definition. The linguistic ideology articulated by Plotinus (and by the later writers cited by Sells) offers a linguistic structure as the true map of a reality hidden, yet ultimately revealed, by language.

Sells creates a discourse of ineffability that universalizes the ancient Greek linguistic ideology and disconnects it from Platonic interpretation. He abandons any remaining notion of the natural connection between names and what they name. This move, in contradistinction to Plato and Plotinus, aligns closely with modern linguistic sensibilities. These sensibilities place the motivated (non-conventional) link with reality just outside language. What exactly is "outside" language not surprisingly meshes with contemporary ideas about truth.

Sells constructs a new discourse about the ineffable that "displaces the grammatical object, affirms a moment of immediacy, a moment of ontological preconstruction" (1994, 9–10). In other words, the speaker is able to reach directly past nouns to a "meaning event" that exists outside language. This meaning event is "transreferential" and in particular is the basis for an experience of truth. Thus the discourse can "evoke in the reader an event that is—in its movement beyond the structures of the self and other, subject and object—structurally analogous to the event of the mystical union" (Sells 1994, 10). Reifying the gap of reference leads to mystical union, something that happens far from the realm of language. Reference must first be broken down, since some things exist that cannot be talked about: "At this moment, the standard referential structures of language are transformed: the breakdown of the reflexive/nonreflexive grammatical distinction in the antecedence of a pronoun it sees it(self) in it(self); the breakdown of the perfect/imperfect distinction (it always has been occurring and always is occurring)" (Sells 1994, 212). The "natural" link undergirding reference, connecting language with reality, is now supplanted by the personal experience of mystical union. This experience forges a connection between people and truth: "This moment in which the transcendent reveals itself as the immanent is the moment of mystical union" (Sells 1994, 212). While it is possible that other routes lead to mystical union, this is the core route for his study. The model can easily be extended beyond whichever specific sources he chooses to site, since the claim can be made that no language is able to encompass reality. Therefore all experiences of truth, in this case the self, are founded on structural negation of negation.

In addition to jettisoning the natural link between name and object, two new aspects of the modern ineffable discourse are particularly striking. First, what is attained only via ineffable discourse is not divinity. Since he is universalizing Plotinus, it is best to avoid reference to a specific divinity. That is, while Basilides and Plotinus had very specific Late Antique ideas about divinity, Sells is seeking something suitable for contemporary debates about mysticism. No specific theological concepts can be used, and the discredited perennial philosophies that lumped distinct religious traditions together must also be avoided. The ineffable now appears to be not so much divinity, as it was for Basilides and Plotinus, but a notion of the Self. The gap of reference is overcome by an experience of the Self's mystical union presumably with some Other, an Other that is usually as distant from it as a word is from the object it refers to.

The second major shift is in the use of this new ineffability. Sells is constructing a discourse about ineffability as part of a scholarly debate about the use of religious experience as evidence for truth claims. Mystical experiences are often presented as proof of an encounter with reality in some form; and if that is to be accepted, the manner in which reality is encountered can then be clarified. Thus the terms *mysticism*, and *mystical experience*, convey the truth implications concept familiar from *miracle* (Proudfoot 1985, 145). If ideas about reference are cultural constructs, the deeper semiotic structure (what is not naming) cannot be dismissed as a cultural construct. This route to truth is possible since minds have universal similarities that can be mapped exactly where language ends.

The context for this modern version of ineffability is academic battles about the status of mystical experiences and whether they are proof of some level of reality.[40] In short, for scholars such as Stephen Katz, all religious experiences are mediated by specific terminology and imagery that outline what is to be encountered (Katz 1978). Thus, a Jewish mystical experience will be completely determined by the terminology of Jewish traditions. If, however, the core of a mystical experience is the encounter with some inexpressible reality beyond language, then that reality is independent of any particular literary or oral tradition. The experience permits an individual to transcend a tradition or culture and have an unmediated encounter with truth (or divinity, or both).

In elevating ineffability to the status of an instrument for proving the validity of mystical experience, Sells goes so far as to claim its moral superiority. If a fashion of ineffability is seen simply as theology, as it was in the ancient world, then both its truth and its moral value are impugned. The "anarchic" (nonreferential) meaning event is reduced in value, which must be avoided. He writes, "To explain away the anarchic moment is to turn apophatic language into conventional theology. Yet to insist upon the integrity of the anarchic moment is to highlight certain moral and intellectual risks" (Sells 1994, 209). The stakes are high, since this fashion of ineffability leads not only to the truth based on a distinct

---

40 As Hollywood points out, "Sells's work seems poised with and against modern and postmodern academic discussions of mysticism" (1995, 565).

theological tradition and experience but to that of other individuals as well. Otherwise, it would be of little scholarly value for evaluating claims about mystical union and would remain only a cultural construct.

The three fashions of ineffability, Basilides, Plotinus, and Sells, all demonstrate the irresistible appeal of language as somehow containing a revelation of truth, even if that truth is defined by the *limits* of language. The three examples all show that ideas of reference and definition undergird the search for truth at the very limits of language. The truth that these investigators find is determined by how they imagine language to work.

The legacy, and the limitations, of Basilides and Plotinus reverberate in Sells's theories. For Basilides and Plotinus, some dimensions of the monotheistic deity were above matter and beyond the representational capacity of materialist language. The best etiquette for speaking about the deity was a fashion of ineffability that preserved deference and permitted a closer approximation of truth and divinity. Neither author was aware of how fully linguistic structures shaped his theology.

Sells presents a universal chronotope of voicing that is completely decontextualized from earlier uses.[41] His notion of ineffability drops the exegetical context of Plotinus and Basilides, grappling with Platonic statements about materiality and creation. It universalizes the Platonic ideology of reference (modified to drop any idea of natural reference). Pointing to the limitations of reference makes the noncontingent reality of mystical union available to everyone, and not just as a result of human intention in any form.

Language can still provide the model of reality, based on the way reference appears to the speaker to work.[42] Sells's fashion of ineffability elevates metasemantic linguistic structures into an ontological description of reality yet the fashion of using descriptive names and of undoing description via reverse description builds upon aspects of language of which "their users have no accurate, conscious, meta-level understanding" (Silverstein 2000, 95). Each model for investigating truth (e. g., nouns, dialogue) is an example of "a conceptual product of the linguistic conditions on which it rests" (Silverstein 2000, 86).

What Sells did not fully realize is how this voicing emerges from decontextualized language ideologies as they are championed by specific historical sources of power. The exegetes had particular roles in the changing landscapes of emerging monotheism in which ancient texts were being reinterpreted. Sells con-

---

41 On a similar decontextualization of a chronotope see Silverstein (2000, 117).

42 As Silverstein explains, "Languages, then, each seem to contain an implicit ontology as a function of structural factors of mapping from/projecting onto the universe of 'reality,' the uniqueness and nonlinguistic manifestation of which become critical issues" (2000, 91).

structs a modern fashion of ineffability by further abstracting the limits of reference from the Platonic linguistic ideology. This new model is needed to shore up recent debates about the validity of mystical experiences and the question of what lessons can be drawn from them. Proudfoot outlines this use of mystical experience as a truth claim, stating, "Ineffability is not a simple unanalyzable characteristic of the experience, as [William] James implies, but ... an artifact of the peculiar grammatical rules that govern the use of certain terms in the religious context" (1985, 125).

Ultimately, Sells inhabits rather than describes the ideology in question. In addition to using (instead of explaining) the ideology, he elevates his theory of ineffability, drawn directly from a language ideology, to a theory of reality. This is a category mistake, conflating a set of epistemological concerns (specifically about the capability of the medium of representation) with a belief about the world. In a circular move, "...the framework of philosophical discourse produces the very picture of subjectivity it was supposed to simply clarify and reveal" (Lee 1997, 225). Truth is still sought, and found, in the realm of linguistic structure.

2 Speech Acts and Divine Names: Comparing Ancient and Modern Linguistic Ideologies of Performativity

Speech-act theory gained immense popularity following John Austin's influential book *How to Do Things with Words* (1962).[1] Austin famously argued that certain first-person statements were not so much truth claims as speech acts, which "do things." His examples include "I now pronounce you man and wife" and "I give and bequeath my watch to my brother." Austin's continuing dominance in discussions of the social construction of culture excludes other ideas about how words relate to their contexts of use. An alternative model for effective language is naming. Christening was one of his examples, but he did not discuss names, since his emphasis was on a set of first-person verbal forms. This chapter begins with some observations about the linguistic role of names and then turns to a series of Jewish explorations and uses of divine names. The final step is to compare these ancient ideas with modern formulations of what is standardly referred to as "performativity."

How Personal Names Name

Uttering personal names is subject to widespread taboos in what appears to be a striking case of cross-cultural agreement. As Luke Fleming explains, "The tabooing of personal names is a frequent and rather salient phenomenon, showing up time and again in ethnographic descriptions" (2011, 142). Something about personal names elicits tremendous concern on the part of speakers. Using a name seems to have implications beyond reference, in the same way that the first-person verbal formulas did not seem to Austin to be primarily about reference. Taboos carefully delineate the social permission needed to use names, outlining how names can and cannot be used in both oral and written form. These taboos result not just from specific and localized ideologies about names. Taboos result from the special role of personal names, including how they are created, their links to contexts of use, and their symbolic meanings.

The "performativity" of names is based on the distinct linguistic role of personal names. Names do not simply refer to individuals. As Saul Kripke argued, personal names refer based on the "baptismal" events when those names are

---

1 See the discussion of Austin in the Introduction, page 4.

https://doi.org/10.1515/9783110768602-003

first "fixed" as referring to particular people (1980, 4). Thus there is a "rigid designation" of names, which permits them to be used in different settings with the same reference (Lee 1997, 224).[2]

Every name is closely related to the specific social context in which it is conferred, encoding all sorts of information about the speakers who endow the name and the addressee who is named. This "pointing-to" or indexical capacity of names is familiar from other context-dependent linguistic units, such as the oft-discussed deictics ("this," "then," etc.).[3] Unlike the noun "cat," for example, which can be easily redefined in different contexts, a personal name carries the same reference across contexts (Fleming 2011, 149). A personal name functions both referentially and indexically, as if stating, "This very specific cat and only this unique cat."

These indexical implications operate across contexts. A personal name is, therefore, "resistant to recontextualization" (Fleming 2011, 149). Citation, for example, cannot diffuse contextual implications. It is hard to talk *about* a name without seeming to use it. Because of the "rigid" reference, personal names cannot be casually employed without invoking complex social implications and so must be hedged with social restrictions. The sources of both a name's "performativity" and its social restriction are the formal and context-related (indexical) capacity of language put into effect by the particular social process of conferring personal names.

The indexical (contextual) implications of names are contagious, carrying over to other lexical units that resemble names. Words that sound like the name may be restricted, as if the sounds of the name were inextricable from the name taboo. Fleming explains, "Homophone and near-homophone avoidance represents an essentialization of the performative effect of verbal taboos as adhering in the material sign-form itself" (Fleming 2011, 157). In some traditions the shape of the name, as an iconic mapping of the name, may also be significant.[4]

A personal name is also a unique symbol. Each name, being an arbitrarily chosen sign, has the potential to be interpreted as symbols are interpreted. As

---

2 As noted by Lee, Kripke was addressing issues of "sense" raised by Frege and offering an alternative solution to the approach taken by Austin, among others (Lee 1997, 222–225).

3 Personal names combine "the constant denotation of the truly symbolic nouns with the indexical denotation of shifters, anaphoric pronouns and demonstratives" (Fleming 2011, 151). On indexes and indexicality, see note 10 in the Introduction.

4 See for example the attempt to preserve the shape of the Hebrew letters in Greek manuscripts. Another example is calling a signature a "John Hancock" because of the size and prominence of his signature on the Declaration of Independence.

an "inherently inferring noun-phrase type," a personal name (whether one lexeme or several) refers uniquely and irrevocably to the person named, even as it stands symbolically for that person (Fleming 2011, 146). Names are minitexts just waiting for symbolic interpretation, and interpreters are eager to take up this task.

We can now outline the different aspects to the inherent "performativity" of personal names. Personal names are not descriptions but are contextually linked from the very start and carry with them a series of subsequent linkings. As Lee explains, "The semantics of proper names is based not on a description model—nor can it be reduced to such a model—but rather on an initial indexical specification backed up by a sociohistorically constructed and transmitted meta-indexical chain of reference" (1997, 90). These links are put into action without any intentionality on the part of the speaker and so offer a model distinct from Austin's speech acts with their felicity conditions.

Divine names, not surprisingly, compound the problems of rigid reference and the indexical implications of personal names, offering particularly rich examples of deference and taboos. As a mode of performativity, divine names are particularly instructive, because unlike Austinian speech acts they highlight the role of indexical icons as motivators of efficacy. Their seemingly natural performativity contrasts with the conventional performativity of speech acts. At the same time, divine-name ideologies implicate other types of signs (writing, art, etc.), opening up the issue of cross-modal efficacy: that is, how signs other than language also have contextual implications (efficacy). As we will see in the examples below, a natural form of performativity also has a contagious potential, which conventional verb-based performativity does not.

Modern analysis of Jewish divine-name traditions toggles between two stances. In the first, Jews were the first people from the ancient world to correctly eschew a personal name for the monotheistic deity as not only unnecessary but also a theological embarrassment.[5] In the second, its obverse, Jewish divine names were so powerful that the Jewish deity who made use of his name was guilty, by modern standards, of engaging in magic.[6] Neither of these explanations (ineffable/magical) accounts for the intricate ways that Jewish exegetes mapped the divine presence via the divine names. A correct understanding of the meaning and use of divine names "simultaneously guards against the worship or reverence of 'idols' but permits representations that are themselves exemplars or analogies of 'semiotic mediators' grounded in the very nature of di-

---

5 For an iteration of this stance, see Stroumsa (2005).
6 For this argument, see Hayman (1989).

vinity (or the cosmos more generally) that have a duality of immanence and transcendence built in" (Leone and Parmentier 2014, S3). Divine names, along with their indexical implications, are available as mediating devices to represent the deity. How these representations work must be clarified by the interpreters. Names have an inherent closeness or summoning capacity that makes balancing talk about divinity against potential misuse of divine names a challenge, as we will see in the examples below.

Example 1: Philo on Divine Names

The first century CE exegete Philo of Alexandria leads us through a more nuanced discussion of divine names, and thus divine effability, than we saw in the previous chapter.[7] Personal names for gods were not a problem in early Greek or Israelite religious texts.[8] The role of a deity's personal name presented challenges in increasingly monotheistic theology.[9] Words that previously described a type of being (a god) now functioned as personal names, as in the shift from a god to God. Philo used divine names as a prism for elaborating an array of major theological points. John Whittaker posits that Philo wanted to claim that the deity was nameless but could not because of the extensive Scriptural divine names (1992, 66).[10] Perhaps, but for Philo every divine name is an intimate representation of some aspect of divinity. Far from being ineffable, this balancing act demanded many, many words.

As outlined in the previous chapter, ancient theorists retained some belief in a natural connection between names and the objects named. Standard naming is mostly based on convention, but that did not exhaust naming. Natural names existed but were limited and the most difficult to investigate. "Socrates ... shows how the relationship between various phonetic realizations and the corresponding 'ideal name' is indeed conventional and arbitrary, while the relationship between the 'ideal name' and the immutable world of form is natural and universal" (Parmentier 1994, 179).

This point lays out the basic path Philo followed. He tracked the origin of words and the potential natural connection between words and their objects.

---

7 See above page 24.
8 See above page 51.
9 Some of them are still seen today in the irregular capitalization of "god" and "God."
10 Including more than three thousand appearances of "YHWH" and numerous lexemes and lexeme-clusters that can be read as names (Elohim, El-Shaddai).

His etymologies, for example, exploit the natural status of word names.[11] Beyond etymologies, he employed two approaches worth looking at in some detail: first, positing a major positive role for the name giver and, second, distinguishing between different divine names and their meanings.

On the first approach, as a good Platonist, Philo was committed to the role of name givers as the originators of at least some names. According to Cratylus, the name giver "is the rarest of craftsmen among men" (*Cratylus* 388 – 389).[12] Others were less sure: "Might the original name makers have been ill informed and encoded their misinformation in the names they coined?" (*Cratylus* 436). Philo happily enters into this discussion, since it is an opportunity to present the superior Jewish name giver Adam. Philo emphasizes that the fit between names and things is perfect, since "the name given and that to which the name is given differ not a whit" (*Cherubim* 56). The Jewish version of the name-giving narrative allots the task to only one person, making it more likely to "bring about harmony between name and thing" (*Alleg. Interp.* 2.15). Adam, who names the animals, is presented as a superior name giver with royal status (*Creation* 148 – 150).[13] Naming was a test to show his wisdom, and he was so successful that the nature of the being was revealed through his naming. Adam realized that he does not truly know his own nature, so he does not name himself (*Alleg Interp.* 1.91– 92). Adam has a name given to him by the deity, who does know Adam's nature. This schema of Name giving sets up a problem for divine names: Who can be the giver of a name to the deity? Divine names can only be known to humans by revelation.

When he turns to his second approach, interpreting divine names, everything becomes more complicated. Philo must balance intricate notions of deference and avoidance with his commitment to the importance of divine names. In Philo's case, the very notion of divine names could be used in multiple ways to make subtle and sometimes confusing points about the divine presence in the mundane world. Instead of being beyond language, for Philo divine names must be talked about from many angles in order for a new divine mediation to emerge. He views each divine name as revealing a facet of the deity; no single name or idea about the meaning of names can encompass all the lessons to be learned. Philo adopts three strategies for the possibilities and problems of interpreting divine names: first, giving divine names interpretive glosses that teach lessons; second, giving new names to divine names; and third, explicitly ad-

---

11 On Philo's etymologies, see Hanson (1967). For the etymologies in Plato, see Sedley (1998).
12 See also *Cratylus* 401 and the discussion in Baxter (1992, 41– 48).
13 See also *Questions and Answers on Genesis* 1.20 – 21. For discussion of Adam as name giver, see Winston (1991, 123 – 125) and Chidester (1992, 32– 33).

dressing extensive restrictions about their use. These strategies are used as needed, depending on what other points he wants to make.

The first strategy for dealing with divine names is glossing them, as if he were writing a dictionary of the meanings of divine names.[14] This interpretive strategy, employed in a number of different exegetical contexts, should not be oversystematized. It is not clear that he was working from a consistent general model. Philo wrote for different types of readers, and his ideas about names do not make a neat package.

Employing a broad linguistic equation, Philo glosses God's name as "word/ λόγος" (*Confusion* 146).[15] This metasemantic (and metapragmatic) equation shakes loose the tight connection between the deity and the name, since "word" refers less rigidly than "name." The move quickly becomes circular when "word" is next equated with (defined as) "name," a step Philo does not make—but others will (Janowitz 1993). The deity's name is described as "specific" (ἴδιος), which Colson translates as "special" (*Abraham* 51).[16] A reference to the "eternal" name appears in *Dreams* 1.229.[17] All these glosses stress new symbolic content for the divine names, pressing toward abstract qualities.

Philo also describes the deity as "not completely nameable" (ἀκατανόμαστος, "beyond complete naming"), and "beyond complete comprehension" (ἀκατάληπτος, *Dreams* 1.67).[18] These are nearly ideal names for the deity, since they are so explicit about the limits of naming.[19] These are good examples of how wordy discussions of "ineffability" can be, since it is useful to comment in detail on the limits of language as somehow being iconic of something about the deity.

These glosses are also very close to being new names for the original divine names. As part of an extended investigation into names (*Names* 11–17), Philo offers a new divine name glossing the enigmatic Hebrew phrase-name "I-am who I-am" (Exodus 3:14) as "my nature is to be, not to be spoken" (*Names* 11).[20] This

---

14 This task is both metasemantic definition and metapragmatic because of the power of divine names.

15 See also "his word [*logos*] is his deed" (*Sacrifices* 65).

16 Translations of Philo throughout are from the Loeb Classical Library edition, Colson and Whitaker translators, cited in the bibliography, with adaptations as noted.

17 A term Philo again contrasts with the "borrowed" name.

18 On these terms, see Whittaker (1983, 306), citing *Tim.* 28 and *Parm.* 142. See also *Moses* (1.75) about the unavailability of an ideal name.

19 On the unknowability of the human mind, which is like the unknowability of the deity, see Philo, *Abraham* 74–76 and *Dreams* 1.30, discussed in Runia (1988).

20 This section of Philo's text is heavily emended, perhaps because it posed challenges to ancient readers (Runia 1988, 76). On the issue of the translation of the Hebrew name into Greek, see the bibliography in Vasileiadis (2014).

extended name focuses attention on something *about* the deity that distinguishes him from other named objects. The new name implies that the speaker is not using the name but is only explaining the noun phrase. This renamed name is a brilliant use of an explicit statement about the functions of words (a metapragmatic statement) that is also a new definition of the name (a metasemantic statement).[21]

In each instance Philo tries to direct the potential meanings and uses of divine names by renaming the deity with names that give greater emphasis to their symbolic meanings. Philo endows the divine name with propositional content, since "personal names, like true symbols, are nomically calibrated" (Fleming 2011, 149). Emphasizing the symbolic content of divine names points to a timeless, nomic aspect of the deity and away from any suspicion that Philo is casually referring to the deity or oversimplifying the implications of divine address.

In his second, closely related strategy, Philo contrasts types of divine names. In his discussion of the name revelation in Exodus 3:14 in *Names* 11, he states that a *kurion* (κύριον) name is not available to humans. Colson translates *kurion* as "personal"; Runia prefers "legitimate."[22] Neither of these translations captures Philo's strategy. A *kurion* name does not merely denote its object; it bears a necessary and essential relation to that object, which is far beyond the notion of "legitimate." The translation "ideal" aligns Philo's naming with the Platonic notion of naming. Philo uses the masculine form of *kurion* later in the same section ("the name 'Lord [κύριος, *kurios*] God,'" *Names* 12), where "Lord" points to the type of name the deity should have and thereby to Philo's idea of a *kurion* name that may better suit divinity (a lordly name for the Lord).

Philo argues that people do not have access to the *kurion* name, but they have access to a name that they can use, according to Colson's translation of *Names* 12, "by license of language" (*katachrēsin*).[23] The translation "borrowed" may capture Philo's point a bit better.[24] A borrowed name will not be expected to be a perfect fit but instead is used based on convention. The gap between it

---

21 See the Introduction for explanations of these terms.

22 Runia considers the translations "legitimate" and "proper," arguing for the former (1988, 76). Aristotle's use of *kurion onoma*, where *kurion* is sometimes translated "normal," "ordinary" (*Rhet.* 3.2, 1404b6, 31, 35, 39), is discussed by (Kennedy 1997, 189) and is sometimes cited, but the usage does not illuminate Philo's linguistic ideology or his high evaluation of the texts that he interprets.

23 As a rhetorical trope, *katachrēsis* employs the name of an object for a second object. Such pseudodefinition is similar to the metasemantic model of the metaphor. Specific contours of comparison can be motivated by pseudodefinitions.

24 See John Whittaker's detailed refutation of Runia's attempt to finely gradate Philo's use of *katachrēsis* (1983).

and what it stands for is obvious, since it is not the ideal name (as in "the lordly name for the Lord").

The same contrast appears in several other treatises. In *Sacrifices* 101, Philo compares the phrase "as a man" from Deuteronomy 1:31, which is used not as "*kurio*-speaking" (*kuriologetai*) but as a "borrowed" manner of speaking (*katachrēsis*). Colson tries to capture the distinction with the contrasting translations "literal" and "as a figure." He is unable, however, to use "literal" consistently, on account of the many different nuances that Philo employs. The basic point is that the phrase "as a man" cannot be an exact fit with divinity; it is needed because of "our feeble apprehension." The same contrasting terms appear in *Abraham* 120, where Philo argues that it is a case of borrowing to state that God has a shadow. This idea cannot be applied to the deity *kuriologesthai*, which Colson and Whitaker translate as "properly," but only as *katachrēsis*: that is, "loose speaking."

Continuing with yet more points made in *Names*, Philo also states, "He allows them to use by borrowing, as though it were his ideal [*kurion*] name, 'Lord [*kurios*] name God,'" (*Names* 12). Colson struggles with this gloss, translating *onoma* (name) as "title," so that the phrase reads "title Lord God." But Philo uses "name," as he is still working with the naming process. He tramples grammar a bit in order to have his renaming work, leaving a text that is disputed and therefore emended.[25] Again, it is not possible to use terms like "literal" and "metaphoric" to describe Philo's exegesis, though the rough overlap of the contemporary metasemantic implications of the terms makes such usage tempting.

Philo's third strategy with divine names is to restrict their use very broadly, as a reflection of their natural power. He emphasizes that divine names are often used, but not often used correctly. Whatever Scriptural constrictions related to the use of the deity's name may have once entailed, Philo introduces new arguments. It is, for example, a sin to pronounce the "most holy" name using a mouth that utters unsuitable words (*Decalogue* 93). Using a divine name must not be done "lightly" (ῥᾳδίως, *Spec. Laws* 2.3).[26] The correct use of a divine name depends on the correct status of the person's soul, adding a complex demand to the qualifications for uttering a divine name. He insists that using a name correctly maps the essence of what is named, making correct use of the

---

25 Colson and Whitaker describe Philo as mixing up the term *kurion onoma* as (1) a noun used in its literal or strict sense and (2) a proper or personal name (Philo LCL 5:149 note a.). Philo is not mixing these ideas up but trying to illustrate how what we think of as literal relates to divine naming when it comes to the capacity of a divine name to represent.

26 This renamed name does not necessarily refer to the Tetragrammaton, in which Philo does not seem particularly interested. On swearing, see also *Spec. Laws* 4.40.

divine name the end result of a long journey. Again, Philo does not claim that the deity has no name, only that his name has to match his essence (and thus his power).

Vows with divine names are just too great an opportunity for Philo to let pass by. A person swearing an oath may know a specific divine name; but that knowledge is superficial. Knowing the name does not necessarily mean knowing the god's essence (*Alleg. Interp.* 3.207–208). The person making the vow does not need to know anything about the deity's essence in order for the vow to work, and vows made with impure mouths may still be considered vows. Such usages prove that the status of the vows' makers is not that of wise initiates. Whether or not a true initiate would ever make a vow using a divine name remains an open question; the name-avoiding initiate is probably an idealized picture, as in Josephus's reference to Essenes, who avoid oaths except for the single powerful one that binds them to their community. According to Josephus's dramatic depiction, they would rather die than utter the divine name (*Jewish War* 2.145).

In an insightful analysis, Maren Niehoff characterizes Philo's ideas about language as a "divine metalanguage" (2001, 188). God's names do not so much constitute a metalanguage, that is, a complete language about language. Instead, Philo's investigation outlines the metasemantic and metapragmatic implications of the deity's mode of speaking. The deity's speech is explicitly demarcated from human speaking not in terms of reference but in terms of contextual implications. At the same time, given the nature of names, these context-related aspects of names also function for human speakers to some extent. As with many of Philo's ideas, this distinction is not presented systematically. Bits and pieces of linguistic ideology are presented in specific exegetical contexts, depending on the textual phrasings he is working with. In *On the Decalogue*, for example, Philo explains that the deity "speaks not utterances but deeds" (*Decalogue* 47).[27] The statement "You saw no similitude but only a voice" (Deuteronomy 4:12) proves that the deity speaks not like humans but in a visible voice. "Words spoken by God are interpreted by the power of sight residing in the soul, whereas those that are divided up among the various parts of speech appeal to hearing" (*Migr.* 49). Linguistic models undergird all human/divine distinctions, and speaking like a deity is one of the signs that Moses was a god (Litwa 2014).

Insofar as Philo is successful in turning names into symbolic statements about the deity, he may appear to have dodged some of the contagion and inher-

---

[27] Philo does not make much of this idea, but it is fundamental to later Jewish exegesis (Janowitz 1993).

ent performativity of divine names. Despite Philo's best efforts to completely re-shape divine names, instituting maximal deference and not mischaracterizing the available names as ideal, he is left with a name that is just as problematic as ever. Each new name may include a commentary about language (metase-mantic statements about the limits of naming) and explicit cautions about use (explicit metapragmatic restrictions). Because of the inherent function of names, the renamed name retains the same rigid reference and indexical impli-cations. Later generations of exegetes of Plato and the Hebrew Scriptures will continue to struggle with divine names. Each new interpretation swill be present-ed as the logical articulation of the basic notion of how names represent and therefore what the text said in the first place.

Example 2: Divine Name as Circumlocution and Text

Divine names loom even larger in our next example. In the rabbinic divine-name ideology, the Genesis Creation story is given a new interpretation: in a baptismal naming event that is hard to top, the deity creates the world by speaking his Name (Janowitz 1993). The divine name, as a synthesis of all creative ability, is itself given a name that refers in shorthand both to the fact that it is a name and to its complex content. The name used to create the world is given the name *Shem ha-Meforash,* an obscure term that can be glossed as "the Exception-al Name."[28] As a Name for the divine name, the term cannot be explained by pin-pointing a unique name to which it refers or by finding the best translation. No doubt, in distinct texts, the term refers to distinct "names," and depending on the text, a variety of arguments can be made about which name is *THE* NAME.

More important, as a Name for the divine name, the term crystallizes in a single unit the ideologies discussed so far. That is, the term signals that the Name itself is now an object of speculation and investigation. The names, by re-ceiving a Name, can each be talked about as a topic. As something to be talked about, the elusive Name that is known only through the many available names can, indeed must, be interpreted in order for it to reveal its secrets.

Not only is the Name a text to be studied, but it is a particularly powerful text. The noun phrase *Shem ha-Meforash* is a shorthand reference for the process of divine naming, both as the Name refers to the deity and as it is an instrument of creativity. Exegesis of the Name is exegesis of all of the deity's power bundled in a single word. The choice of name is obvious, again, following linguistic ideol-

---

28 Other possible translations include the Explicit Name and the Special/Preeminent Name.

ogy: the name is the word that most closely "stands for" the deity. This ideology, as noted in Chapter One, departs substantially from ancient Israelite principles. There were no injunctions against merely stating the name. Similarly, while the creativity of God's name is mentioned in a few Scriptural references, nowhere is it explicitly stated that the deity created the world by speaking his Name.

A particularly rich anecdote revealing the new linguistic ideology states that the divine name was not supposed to be uttered even in court by a witness to blasphemy.[29] As to the definitional limits of the names—Are all words used to refer to the deity "names"?—some would extend punishment for blasphemy even to those who substituted divine attributes for the Name, giving the attributes Name status (b. Sanhedrin 56a).

The creative power of the Name was harnessed by select biblical figures, who used it for protection and even violent acts of aggression.[30] The divine name was also used to animate lifeless images, a variation on the Creation theme.[31] An entire history—or rather, a series of conflicting histories—of the Name was composed. The distant past and the future were both portrayed as times when people knew (or would know) how to use the Name, as the history of the Name became a metaphor for the presence of the deity on Earth and for his interaction with his people. One anecdote, for example, states that the Name was once entrusted to the entire nation, given to them during their journey through the desert. It was taken away, however, when they worshipped the Golden Calf.[32] Perhaps the most famous "history" is that at one time the Name was widely known, but growing corruption led to increasing restrictions, until the Name was not used any more.[33] Despite its loss, the divine name was said to be used in an obscure but dramatic Talmudic anecdote about the creation of a calf by rabbis (b. Sanhedrin 65a).

This model of the name has implications for both ritual and interpretation. An analogy has been established between Name and text; simply put, since the Name can be a text, a text can be a Name.[34] The named Name is now the icon by which all verbal expressions are measured and judged. The Scriptural text de-

---

29 Sanhedrin 7:5 and b. Sanhedrin 91a. Compare b. Sanhedrin 55a.
30 Solomon uses a ring with the Name on it to subdue a demon (b. Gittin 68b). Moses kills an Egyptian with the Name (Exodus Rabba 2:14).
31 Later popularized in the golem stories. See also the Opening of the Mouth Ceremony in the next chapter.
32 Song of Songs Rabba 7:9 on Exodus 33:6. B. Sotah 47a.
33 B. Yoma 39b, jYoma 40d, iii, 7. In the present world, prayers are not heard because they do not include the Name (Midrash on Psalms 91).
34 For the Torah as a collection of divine names, see Idel (1981).

rives its value from the extent to which it is a copy of this model. Exegesis of the Torah, a collection of names, that is, of potentially creative words, demands investigation of both semantic and nonsemantic elements. Rabbinic exegetical literature will be dotted with metaphors and anecdotes that try to make this point. For example, the idea that the addition or subtraction of a single letter will destroy the world calls attention to the power of the text and its pragmatic implications.[35] Other stories recount the necessity of rearranging the manifest content in order to find the other, hidden content.[36] The "nameness" of the text not only is evident on the surface but exists as an exegetical possibility.

The name ideology is read back into the biblical text via the Aramaic translation. For example, the revelation of the divine name in Exodus 3:14–15 is expanded. The Hebrew text reads:

> Moses said to the Lord, ... 'Who should I say sent me?'
> And the Lord said to Moses, I am who *I am*.
> And he said, And this you will say to the children of Israel: 'I am' sent me. (Exodus 3:14–15, emphasis added)

In the Aramaic translation, the name is greatly expanded:

> And Moses said to the Lord, 'Who should I say sent me?'
> And the Lord said to Moses, I am who I am.
> And then he said, *And thus you will say to the children of Israel: 'The one who spoke and the world was there at the beginning, and who is to speak to it, "exist," and it will exist, sent me'.* (Targum Neofiti Exodus 3:14–15, emphasis added)[37]

The implicit claim of this translation of God's revelation of his name in Exodus is that the new (Aramaic) version has the same meaning as the original (Hebrew) text. In the translation, however, the deity has a new name. If we compare the Hebrew original with the Aramaic translation we find that the Aramaic has expanded the deity's name from the simple "I am" to the more complex "The one who spoke ..." The deity's revelation of his name to Moses is a choice opportunity for interpretation. Names present ready-made hidden texts for the exegetes, in that the semantic content of names can often be explained in a variety of

---

35 Attributed to Rabbi Ishmael in b. Erubim. See Scholem (1965, 39).

36 If the correct order had been given, anyone could use it to wake the dead or performs miracles (Midrash on Psalms 3:2).

37 Targum Neofiti is dated anywhere between the second and the fifth century CE. This translation is from the edition of (Diez Macho 1968). The Targumic ideology of the divine name is presupposed by the rabbinic exegetical texts (third century–eighth century CE).

ways. Proper names logically may lack obvious semantic content: that is, no meanings that emerge systematically from linguistic structure. Meanings can, however, be supplied by the exegetes. Every name is waiting to be explained. As we saw in the case of Philo, few exegetes can refrain from discussing names.

The text in Exodus seems already to contain a short meditation on the meaning of God's name, playing with the connection between the name YHWH and the root "be" (*hwh*). The interpretation is then extended in the Aramaic translation. God not only exists himself; he is also the source of all existence as the creator of the world. Thus, in order to refer to him and to explain who he is, the simplest way is to describe him in his unique role as the speaker who creates. The deity's creative act of speaking has become his proper name.

The new name refers to the deity—that is, it points him out as the speaker—and it also predicates something about him as a speaker: that he can speak in this extraordinary manner. The name is thus a short meditation on the notion of divine language; language with a special status because it was spoken by the deity. Humans can say what they want; they speak mere words.

The name of the deity is presented as reported speech or, to put it more correctly, as a report of a report of reported speech. The fact that the Name includes reported speech is no accident. The Scriptural text consists largely of the deity's words reported by Moses.

The linguistic ideology of the Name is evident throughout the Targumic translation. The Aramaic word for "word" (*memra*) is often added in the translation: for example, "I will be there, my *memra*, with you" (Targum Neofiti Exodus 3:12). The introduction of this word is the repeated articulation of an exegetical principle extracted from the very structure of the text. As the Targumic ideology highlights for us with its emphasis on the divine word, the text physically embodies these divine words. Divine speech, in the objectified state of THE TEXT ITSELF, embodies the deity on Earth. The translation, each time it focuses on God's word on Earth, tries to incorporate back into the text the implicit claim of the text, that God's words work (create) on Earth. Because the deity's words are present in the Torah, the words of the text are not just any collection of words but are the words operative in the midst of the community. The word as divine presence physically sits in front of them in the scrolls, which contain actual tokens (examples) of divine speech.[38]

This new version of cross-modal representation of divinity mixes a very delicate, deferential avoidance of the divine name with a very dramatic materializa-

---

38 To argue that the insertion of *memra* is due to the wish to avoid anthropomorphism misses these points (Klein 1982).

tion of it in the form of the physical text. The Name is entextualized into a text that becomes one extended name.[39] Although the entire world is a materialization of the deity, the text (the written divine name) is a much more direct materialization. Divine speech, in the objectified state of the text itself, embodies the deity on Earth.

The Name is a report of a report of a reported speech. Moses reports what the deity told Moses to report and that in turn is the report that the deity told Moses to report. But because of the rigid reference of naming, the text as name can become problematic. The second line of development dilutes the text-as-name, equating divine speech more generally with "word." This equation is a less direct sanctification than the divine name, with fewer implications.[40] The words by which the world was created are found in the document, along with many other examples of divine speech (words). Each "Thus says the Lord" is an utterance of divine speech, and the text is a collection of all such words.

Example 3: The Divine Name in Water

In our next example, divine names take on a dramatic role in a rite that is already dramatic to start with. The *Sotah* (Suspected Adulteress) rite in Numbers 5:11–17, reimagined in subsequent historical periods, is an excellent example of shifting divine-name pragmatics. In a medieval version of the ritual, the two basic signs—words and water with dust in it—are given new semiotic meanings as the ancient text is rethought through the prism of divine naming.

In bare outline the rite in Numbers is as follows: a sacrificial offering of barley flour (not mixed with oil) is presented to the deity; the woman's hair is uncovered; holy water is mixed with dust from the floor of the sanctuary; the priest recites an oath (no specific oath is included in the text); the woman repeats the word "Amen" twice; the priest dissolves written curses in the water; and the woman drinks the "bitter" water; the priest reports that the "water and curses" will cause her "belly to distend" and her "thigh to sag" if she is guilty. The priestly roles are awkward additions to a ritual that did not include them in earlier versions (Milgrom 1999). The drinking of curses, the term "holy water," and the use

---

39 For the Torah as a collection of names, see note 32. For entexualization, see Silverstein and Urban (1996, 1–6 and passim).

40 The opening to the Gospel of John, for example, has to explicitly equate the word (*logos*) with the name God in order to achieve the rigid reference of naming. See Philo's use of this equation cited above, page 35.

of sanctuary dust are unique to this rite.[41] Before turning to the main focus, a later reworking of the rite, it is worth noting that in this rite the woman incorporates curses and holy water that turn her body into a "golden indexical" of divine power (Parmentier 1997, 77).

This rite is reworked in a fascinating medieval version of the ritual found in genizah fragments.[42] The new version is precious evidence of how the metapragmatic basis shifts with new ideas about divine names. In basic outline, the text includes (1) a condensed history of the divine Names (used in Creation and passed down by angels to humans), (2) an explanation of the Names' roles (how they function in the *Sotah* rite), (3) a presentation of the Names, and (4) an explanation of the current form of the rite (what we do now and why it works) and an appended comment on the elevated status of the officiant (like an angel and a High Priest).

Here is a dramatic instance of "the interpenetrations of textual with extra-textual factors" (Hanks 1989, 105). It is nearly impossible to separate out the rite from the metapragmatic commentary mixed in with it. Presumably, just as earlier versions of ordeals that lacked the priestly formulas probably looked suspicious to the priestly editors, the redactors of this version introduced new ideas about divine causation and the human officiant. In order to make the ritual work, an alternative to priestly status is presented and the liturgy is repragmatized with a new mode of divine representation.

The divine Name in the rite functions as the central, self-performing, linguistic form and thus as the basis of the ritual efficacy. This rite has a very particular notion of calling upon the deity's name. The genizah text opens with the formula "Blessed is the name of glory of his kingdom forever and ever."[43] This blessing formula is a clear example of the way certain linguistic forms "laminate all four areas [i. e., linguistic, metalinguistic, pragmatic, and metapragmatic] on top of one another" (Sanders 2004, 170). Invoking the blessed Name is a human appropriation of a divine prerogative by the legerdemain of reported speech. Like forms of politeness that imply obligations of those toward whom the words are directed, each declaration of the blessedness of the name presupposes that the source of blessings (the deity) has already done the blessing. The

---

41 The special powers of dirt are mentioned in Swartz (2002), though in this ritual it is not dirt in general but dirt from the Tabernacle.

42 According to Peter Schäfer, the fragments were probably written in the eleventh or twelfth century (1996, 542). See also Swartz (2002).

43 In the most basic Jewish prayer formula, the blessedness of the name is invoked, instantiating the blessedness of the one whose name it is. On the historical emergence of this formula in rabbinic circles, see Kimelman (2005).

human speaker is simply pointing this out, but the act of pointing it out is a form of received performativity.

The text follows this usage with another linguistic form that operates from a modified metapragmatic stance: the direct uttering of divine Names. Here the one whose name is blessed is invoked in the third person. This may seem to be a less direct invocation than "you," but because of the encoding of divine power in the divine Name, it is a parallel mode of pointing to divine power and putting it into action. It is misguided to say that only a certain type of person—let alone a disparaged magician—adopts this type of metapragmatics, since the power of the divine Name is so central to Jewish theology. What separates this text from other liturgical forms is the fact that this text has obsessive concerns about efficacy of a different sort than we saw with the priests. This is a moment requiring explication and elaboration. Names are fussed with as if to say: the power of the divine Names is not a simple issue of one or two letters but instead is so mystifying and so complicated that it is almost beyond even us (and is surely beyond you). The story of passing down the name is a narrative presentation of efficacy that encodes the secrecy, raising the fascinating issue of the role of secrecy in religion—much beyond the scope of this chapter.[44] The claim to secrecy is itself part of the metapragmatics.

The use of the written curses dissolved in water has also been reinterpreted, since they too have been subordinated—not to the priest but to the divine Name. All self-enacting power is now the power of the divine Name, both written and spoken. Whereas biblical texts seem to have limited theories of effective human speech, this interpretation of the rite seems to have a very limited theory of effective sacred acts. That is, the divine Name threatens to displace all sacred acts, leading to a ritual in which the actions (adding dust, drinking water) are subordinated to the words (and specifically to the divine Name).

In this version of the *Sotah* rite the power of the entire priestly system accrues to the person performing the rite, who is now able, as a divine figure himself, to carry it out. Without this status, the rite cannot be effective. The ordeal depends not only on the deity but also on the divine status of the officiant. This claim does not of course mean that every person thought he was a deity, or even that practitioners did not preserve some dimension of difference between their status and that of the deity.[45] It does mean, however, that the priestly caste

---

44 Some of the central themes are outlined in H. Urban (2006).
45 On the etiquette that demands keeping some hierarchical distinction between various types of divine figures and the deity, see Chazon (2000).

has been replaced by individuals who earn their special status by knowledge of the divine name and how to use it.

Example 4: The Divine Name Over Water

A second example of a rite employing the divine name is from *The Book of the Name*, written by Eleazer of Worms at the beginning of the thirteenth century.[46] The author presents secret doctrines that he hoped to preserve in the face of the death of his teacher and of attacks on the Jewish community.[47] The text begins, "With the Name Was, Is, and Will be, I begin the Book of the Name" (1:1). The name is both the subject of the text and also invoked at the outset. In a sense, the book could end here. As repeated explicitly throughout the treatise, "his name is his reality." If we could see immediately into the name, if we could uncover its structure, all the rest of the text would be commentary. But since we cannot do this, the author explicates the name for us. "Why is the yod at the start of the name?" The answer Eleazer gives is that "Aleph is above, Beth is below, etc.; Yod is afterwards." His name begins with "afterward" in order "to teach that the existence after the world is like that before the world" (2:10).

The text details a ritual for passing on the secret divine name from rabbi to student. Based on Psalm 27:3, "The voice of God is over the waters," the teacher and his students are told to fast and then stand in water up to their ankles.

The rabbi then recites the blessing:

> Blessed are you, our God, the king of the universe, the Lord God of Israel. You are one, and your name is one. You have commanded us to keep your name hidden because it is so terrifying. Blessed are you, and blessed is your glorious name forever, the numinous name of the Lord our God. The voice of the Lord is upon the waters. Blessed are you, our Lord who reveals His secret to those who worship Him, the One who knows all secrets.

The ritual builds in numerous formal (iconic) representations of the deity. In the Genesis Creation story, the deity hovered over the waters in the act of Creation (Gen 1:1). In this version Eleazer uses his secret name, which is hidden from everyone in the world except those worthy to know it. In the ritual, a close identification is made between the divine presence hovering over the waters to create

---

46 This text is not available in English translation or even in a critical Hebrew edition. For a general introduction with some excerpts, see Dan (1995). Translations are my own, adapted from Dan (1995).

47 For information about Eleazer of Worms, see Dan (1995).

the world and the rabbi with his disciples standing in water and uttering the same word. The disciple who participates in the ceremony also knows the name, hearing it just as it was spoken at the moment of Creation. This is a wonderful example of building not only a cosmology but also a cosmogony into a ritual. Recreating the primordial moment of Creation transforms the human speaker.

The fact that the deity has a secret name was widely disseminated. A secret has no social valence if it is not known to exist and to be available to certain people (H. Urban 2003). A rich set of stories elaborates a history for the secret name passed on by priests and then worthy rabbis. Eleazer of Worms revealed this secret only because of the dire circumstances of his life.

The text also describes a miniature version of a ritual carried out after the water ritual at the synagogue, with the divine name recited over a glass of water, paralleling the *Sotah* rite. This recitation of the name over water brings the creative divine power of the name directly into the synagogue. This iconic presentation collapses the ritual into the cosmological time of the original recitation of the name over water and all other similar recitations. This setting for recitation of the name is still available—in fact easily available—after the creation of the world and that primordial use of the divine name.

The recitation over water is a fascinating case of a specific recontextualizing of the name, yet another cross-modal investigation of divine power that combines verbal and nonverbal signs. Just as the name can be represented by a particular building or by a text, in this ritual the name is located "above" water. The water points to the power of the name and vice versa. Together the water and name are a formal representation of the power of the divine name with "performative" force.

Comparing Effective Language

Austin's speech-act theory continues to dominate debates about effective language even as performativity becomes a general explanation for any and all forms of the social construction of culture. It drives out other notions of the context-related dimension of signs in general and language specifically. As one example, in *Excitable Speech*, Judith Butler (1997b, 31–37) favors Austin's model over what Althusser called the "Christian Religious Ideology" of naming. Louis Althusser was interested in "social interpellation," how a person becomes a subject of the state (1994). Althusser turned to Exodus because of the importance of naming ideologies in biblical and postbiblical texts. He introduced, but only briefly, some of the issues involved not only in divine names but in naming in general, putting his finger on something important about the social use of names. Althusser was interested in the deity's name "I am who I am" and its role in establishing him as the ultimate subject. In Christian divine naming, as briefly presented by Althusser, the deity calls out a name, such as "Peter," and thereby turns Peter into a subject. Althusser's primary example of Christian naming ideology is taken from Exodus (3:4,14), where Moses replies "It is I" to God's summons. Moses's reply is followed by the deity's revelation of his name (Exodus 3:4,14). For Althusser, the deity presents himself as the "subject par excellence," just as Moses recognizes that he is a subject of the deity (1994, 134).[48]

From Butler's point of view, naming is a model of limited value, since it depends on the possession of sovereign power by the speaker. This power occurs very rarely in society at large. Equivalent linguistic power operates only in those situations where speech is backed by state forces. She explains, "Human speech rarely mimes that divine effect except in the cases where the speech is backed by state power, that of a judge, the immigration authority, or the police, and even then, there does sometimes exist recourse to refute that power" (Butler 1997b, 32).

Butler is correct that a name can be refused. But the baptismal event plus the rigid reference of names makes it harder to say, "Who? Me?" (Butler 1997b, 33). Butler dismisses Althusser's insights into effective language too quickly. Althusser has revealed another way in which language effects the context of use, one that is not based on the verbs that dominate Austin's theory. Instead divine naming presents a very different concept, based on something about the power of names and naming in general. Both ideologies, speech-act theory and divine naming, offer partial windows into the multifunctionality of language. They differ in the way that language uses are plumbed in search of context-relating social efficacy.

The two linguistic ideologies overlap and differ in striking ways. From one point of view, speech-act performatives could be thought of as themselves a kind of naming; the verbs transparently name the type of action being enacted: "I baptize" is *eo ipso* a baptism. It is this very self-naming that drew Austin's attention in the first place. Since they name an action done by language, they are examples of Silverstein's explicit metapragmatics (1976).[49]

---

48 The naming creates a subject who is subsequently subjected to a greater subject. They mutually recognize each other and also guarantee that "everything is really so" (Althusser 1994, 135).

49 This is why speech acts cannot model all the various functionalities of language but are limited to nameable actions.

Austin's dependence on the self-naming verbs means he has to incorporate enough of the context to demonstrate how a particular verb was understood to encode social action in a particular setting. He had to add felicity conditions in an attempt to locate the context in which a verb is effective and the naming of the action successful. Thus speech-act theory "emerges from a sociohistorically specific formulation from within a culture caught at a particular happenstance moment of lexicalization of certain metapragmatic verbs (verbs used to denote discursive interactional event types) which, as lexical primes, come into and go out of general use" (Silverstein 2010, 344). On the other hand, with their rigid reference names supply a different model of the indexical summoning of the divine presence. No felicity conditions are needed here. Automatic efficacy is taken for granted, and extreme caution must therefore be observed. "The indexical dimension of reference always runs the risk of being converted into an all too explicit performativity" (Fleming 2011, 146).

This Name ideology plays out in numerous ways. Evolving constraints necessitate a constantly shifting calibration of the iconic presentation, ending up with the need to completely obscure the name. As a mediator between humans and their deity, the divine Name is under constant pressure. As Massimo Leone and Richard Parmentier note, "Cross-cultural investigations suggest ... that the greater the assumed unbridgeability of the gap between earthly and transcendent realms ... the more difficult becomes the task of traditional 'semiotic mediators' between realms, mediators that can now become increasingly open to intense ideological critique and political attack" (2014, S8). The advantage of divine names is that their rigid reference helps to bridge that gap.

Yet even as the ideological critique unfolds, the necessary indexical connection that is at the heart of the naming ideology continues to depend upon a material form in order to successfully invoke a divine presence. The material formal representation is always iconically connected to the divine referent. The formal shape is assumed to have a natural rather than a conventional link to the divine. Thus, all our examples of divine-name rituals are built from not only words but other iconic signs as well (reciting the name over water).

One person's formal representation of divinity is another person's idol, even as all representations refer to the deity indexically as they cross-contextually manifest the divine presence in a particular location. The contagion of the natural connection of a name is harder to contain than the efficacy of a conventional speech act, easily dethroned by a mere shift in the verbal form. Both ideologies capture a dimension of the power of language that speakers sense: the capacity of names to invoke a presence and of self-reflexive verbs to describe the very action that they enact.

3 Creating the Forbidden Sign: Ancient and Modern Debates about Proper Representation

The meaning of a religious object used in a ritual easily becomes contentious. Writers defend ritual processes with very specific ideas of exactly how representation *should* work (Parmentier 2009, 149). Competing social groups champion their distinct liturgical practices and the material representations of divinity that the practices depend on. Critics and supporters try to make clear distinctions between proper and improper practices, despite a very muddy reality.

This chapter turns to a range of religious objects that raise special dilemmas of interpretation. The examples, all of which include divine names, are cross-modal (both verbal and non-verbal signs). These examples of overlapping verbal and non-verbal divine representations present a wide variation of sign use, sometimes from the same ritual setting. Some of them are provocative to modern researchers. These usages were probably emmeshed in controversies from the start. Though the most ancient criticisms are lost to us, some viewers probably attacked cave paintings as inappropriate. An additional problem is that modern readers too often cherry-pick ancient polemical texts for terms used in condemnation and retort, hoping to decontextualize the terms and build abstract theories about proper/improper representation. The examples in this chapter demonstrate the futility of many of these appropriations.

Example 1: The Elusive Indexicality of Sacred Spaces (Human Form)

The first example of a multi-layered use of divine representations is two Iron Age drawings on storage jars found at Horvat Teman, an ancient crossroads on the Judah-Sinai border.[1] This striking archaeological find includes two fragmentary drawings with inscriptions which have elicited extensive discussion. In the first drawing (Scene A), an ornate humanoid male and female couple stand between two musicians and a cow with calf.[2] Writing overlaps the figures as fol-

---

[1] The evidence is presented, and one interpretation offered, in Meshel (2012).
[2] For the drawing see Meshel (2012, 87) and Schmidt (2016, 28).

https://doi.org/10.1515/9783110768602-004

lows: Speak to Yaheli, and to Yo'asa and to [...], "I have [b]lessed you before/to Yahweh of Shomron and his Asherah" (Inscription 3.1).[3]

The second drawing (B) includes a small crowd of worshippers near an animal.[4] This scene is also overlapped by an inscription as follows (Inscription 3.9): "to YHWH of Teman and his Asherah [...], whatever he asks from a man, that man, will give him generously. And if he would urge, YHW will give him according to his wishes ..." (Schmidt 2016, 47, 74).[5] A vertical inscription from the same scene reads (Inscription 3.6): "May it go well for you. I have blessed you by YHWH of Teman and by his Asherah. May they (YHWH and Asherah) bless you and may they keep you and may the people of the Lord be [... forever]" (Schmidt 2016, 78).[6]

The role of objects and images in ancient Israelite cult has changed dramatically in the past decades. The old model of aniconic religion has been turned on its head (Hurowitz 2012). First Temple Judahite practices are now seen as being no more aniconic than those of neighboring cultures (Uehlinger 1997). This rethinking is due to the rich archaeological finds and a closer analysis of the rich terminology for cultic practices preserved in Scriptural texts. Numerous objects used in processions, libations, and sacrifices have been discovered (Niehr 1997). Archeological finds include human and animal depictions in metal, ivory, terracotta, and faience, and a variety of types of cylinder seals and clay figurines, sometimes seated on a couch (Uehlinger 1997, 149–152). The theological importance of all these objects does not reflect a narrow subset of cult, as for example, afterlife or fertility (van der Toorn 2002).[7] These practices point to a range of settings and possible contexts of use, not assimilations, lower-class, or foreign cults.[8] Instead contexts of use include enclosed temples, open-air sanctuaries, altars in homes, and personal religious items.

At the same time that the archaeological finds are challenging the once-standard idea that ancient Israelite cult included few images, Scriptural discourse about images is being re-examined.[9] A small selection of biblical texts no longer

---

3 The translation is from Schmidt (2016, 78–79). See also Meshel (2012, 87). Among the many discussions of Asherah, see the classic works by Olyan (1988) and Ackerman (1992). See also note 10 below.
4 For the drawing see Meshel (2012, 92) and Schmidt (2016, 40).
5 Compare Meshel (2012, 98).
6 Compare Meshel (2012, 95).
7 See Uehlinger (1997, 101) and van der Toorn (2002).
8 For example, Moshe Barasch's claim that the use of statues reflects popular religion whereas elites disdain the practice (Barasch 1992).
9 According to Assmann, the sharp distinction between friend and Egyptian foe in the Decalogue necessitates a rejection of images as idolatry (Assmann 1997). *Pace* Assmann, the com-

defines ancient ideas about images. Texts that attacks specific imagery are also dated to a later period, late pre-exilic or exilic (Niehr 1997, 75). A quick survey of cultic terms from Scriptural texts gives a window onto a rich array of lost or partially-repressed objects that were used in lost rituals: *Asherah* (female consort; pole),[10] *massabot* (pillars),[11] *teraphim* (humanoid figures),[12] *cheruvim* (hybrid beasts who carry the throne),[13] *pesel* (sculpted image),[14] *massekhah* (molten image),[15] *ephod* (some form of breastplate),[16] and the *aron* (ark).[17] The infamous golden calves reflected ancient and long-standing practices of depicting the deity in the form of a bull and members of his entourage in the form of animal hybrids (Exodus 32–34).[18] The serpent image (Nehustan 2 Kings 18:4) attributed to Moses was reported to still be used during the reign of Hezekiah, and even then its association with Moses was not questioned (Olyan 1988, 70).

As a quick side note, these terms for objects and rites left a complex heritage that later translators had to struggle with. The modes of production and practices were obscure to later readers and translators. The mystifying biblical vocabulary had to be interpreted in order to be rhetorically useful in later centuries. The English term "idol" is borrowed from the Greek *eidōlon*, which had no negative connotation (Kennedy 1994, 198). Numerous Hebrew words for objects were translated *eidōlon* in the Septuagint, but not all (Kennedy 1994, 199).[19] The Septuagint

---

mandments do not necessarily argue for a rejection of images because they are false (Tugendhaft 2012, 305).

10 *Asherah*, which was probably originally the name of Yahweh's consort, is commonly translated "sacred pole" for the reasons discussed in this chapter. See 1 Kgs 14:15, 14:23, 16:33; 2 Kgs 17:10, 17:16, 21:1–7; and 2 Chr 33:3.

11 This obscure term may refer to some type of burial marker (Gen 35:19–21; 2 Sam 18:18), a stump of a tree or other architectural feature (Isa 6:13, Ezek 26:11), something erected upon the completion of a covenant agreement (Gen 31:51–52, Exod 24:3–8), something translated "obelisk" (Jer 43:13), or something associated with *asherim* (Exod 34:13). See also Lev 26:1 and Hos 3:4.

12 For shifting ideas of how to interpret this term, see van der Toorn (1990).

13 Ezek 1:5–13, 10:14; 1 Sam 4:4; 2 Sam 6:2; Isa 37:16.

14 These may have been metal-covered statues (van der Toorn 2002).

15 Often translated as some form of molten or cast metal statue, as in Judges 17:4.

16 Interpretations range from a breastplate (Exod 28:6–8) to a device used to submit inquiries to the deity (1 Sam 23:6–12) or a statue of some sort (Judg 8:26–27).

17 The Ark was said to contain a number of items, including perhaps statues. See Dick (2005, 59) and van der Toorn (1997, 242).

18 See 1 Kgs 12:28–30; 2 Kgs 10:29, 17:16; Exod 32; Hos 8:5, 13:2 and Olyan (1988, 31).

19 Some, such as *mskh* and *msbh*, were translated into other Greek terms. The term *pesel* is translated five times as "idol" and other times by a Greek term for a carved image ξόανον, *xoanon* (Kennedy 1994, 200).

translators appear to have thrown up their hands and given up on a more consistent translation.

Returning to Scene A, much ink has been spilt in identifying the figures. The
male deity's crown in Scene A is similar to the one worn by the deity Bes; divine
attributes were shared between cults in both verbal and artistic presentations.
Modern viewers face the same challenges of identification ancient viewers
faced. In those cases where a statue is found without a naming inscription or distinct attributes associated with the deity, specific identification is difficult. Morton Smith (1952) emphasized the attribution of jealousy as the single character-
ization that distinguished Yahweh from other ancient Near Eastern gods, an
attribute that would be difficult to portray as part of an image. Labels serve a
vital role, since the ancient viewer needed some help (as does the modern) distinguishing between the distinct deities that might be depicted in a setting such
as the ancient caravan route.

Schmidt judiciously identifies the male figure as YHWH, stating that this
identification "requires far less convoluted arguments than any alternative interpretation offered to date" (Schmidt 2002, 107).[20] The explicit identification is not
part of the original drawing, but someone in the ancient setting made that identification. Deities were also connected to specific locations; hence the full name
of the deity is Yahweh of Shomron/Teman.

In an astute analysis, Schmidt argues that Scene B is an example of "empty
space aniconism" (Schmidt 2002, 114).[21] The scene appears to depict a ritual. The
deity who dwells in the sky is the focus of the worshippers who direct their prayers to that empty space. This use of empty-space aniconism "highlights for the
ancient viewer the transcendence of Yahweh and his Asherah, who invisibly
dwell in the heavens exercising their power to bless those who send homage
to them" (Schmidt 2002, 114).

These distinct sets of images may indicate different ritual contexts. The
drawing points toward the existence of parallel formal hominoid representations
such as statues. Statues were employed in urban cultic centers. Scene A may be
linked to the use of statues in urban temples. A linkage between statues and
Temples is familiar, related to ancient ideas of Temples as houses for the
gods. On the other hand, Scene B may link to the open-air empty-space sanctuaries, another common model of sacred space found in many narratives. In this

---

20 Meshel disassociates the drawings from the inscriptions in order to preserve an image-free
ancient Israelite religion. "There is no support for the idea that the people of Ajrud tried to represent the effigy of YHWH. The drawings on the pithoi do not challenge the accepted view of the
non-iconographic character of Yahwistic cult and theology" (Meshel 2012, 129).
21 Schmidt is adopting the term from Mettinger (1982 and 2006).

cultic setting, instead of statues, verbal formulas or other types of ritual actions invoke the presence of that deity.

Both drawings employ an aesthetic of "overlapping perspective" (Schmidt 2002). Understanding this mode of representation is necessary for the viewer to correctly interpret the scenes. Objects are portrayed from more than one direction at the same time in order to give them three-dimensionality. Ancient viewers understood this social convention and used it to interpret the pictures.[22]

The inscriptions introduce ritual formulas, another mode for creating sacred space. The phrase "I blessed you" from Scene B is compared with Judges 17:2, where a mother declares: "Blessed to YHWH [be] my son" (Meshel 2012, 127).[23] She calls attention to the status of her son as being in a particular state in relation to the deity.[24] Blessings as well as curses are automatically effective speech spoken by the deity but conveyed via human speakers (and even animals). The blessing ultimately comes from the deity. Humans declare other humans blessed as a way of marking the exalted status of the deities and drawing attention to the activity of the deities in the earthly world. The deity is referred to in the third person ("he") and with the personal name (YHWH). Unlike the later rabbinic blessing formula ("Blessed are you, God"), second-person references are made only to the person in the blessed state. The use of "my lord"—for example, by Abraham when greeting the angelic messengers as "My lords"—shows another deferential mode of discourse, used with people who may be of higher status (Genesis 18:3). The same deference was used with a deity by combining the deferential phrase with the personal name.

The overlapping of perspectives is subject to the additional overlapping that connects the two modalities of verbal (inscription) and nonverbal (drawing) and creates an "in front of" location. The blessing takes place before Yahweh and his Asherah (Scene A), or the worshippers (Scene B), literally in the nexus between the words and the drawings before the viewer. The inscriptions call upon the deity and his Asherah to bless specific individuals. The act of blessing indexically ties the representations of divinity (figures and names) in space and time with the worshippers, who are formal (figures and names) models of the blessed.

Multi-modal creation of sacred space happens in many forms. The deity's name may "dwell" in a specific location by means of a statue, by inscribing

---

22 Compare the Egyptian use of size as a sign of divinity.

23 While some English translations offer "by," the Hebrew is not agentive and is better glossed with the sense of "[in relation] to" the deity.

24 As Seth Sanders has demonstrated, in West Semitic languages, the perfective form "I blessed" will be the closest equivalent to the performative, since it is the "morphologically and semantically minimal verbal category" (Sanders 2004, 170).

the name on a monument, and by a foundation sacrifice in which the divine name was deposited (baptismally!) in a temple foundation in written form (Richter 2002, 127–205). In all these cases the specific name of the deity is central, since it refers to exactly which deity is sacralizing the temple, supporting the king, or laying claim to territory. Deuteronomy 12:11 states: "Then to the place the Lord your God will choose as a dwelling place for his Name, there are you to bring everything I command you."[25] The dwelling formula is glossed in several places in Deuteronomy as "to place in" as a clarification of what it means for a name to dwell.[26] The Deuteronomic name-ideology posits the tightest possible knot between the two modalities for representing divinity, verbal and nonverbal: nothing can stand for the deity more directly than his name and thus his building. Like the Iron Age drawings with their inscriptions, the dwelling name-ideology is another example of cross-modal representation. The linguistic model of name is used to calibrate the sacredness of the temple building.[27] The value of the building-as-name ideology activates the special functionality of names.[28] As discussed above, a name has a special relationship with what it names.[29] Each reminder about the indwelling name baptizes the temple in a re-naming event that is itself a repetition of the primordial naming of the deity. Baptism and rebaptism are always indexical, sanctifying the building directly as it connects divine name and place.

Example 2: The Opening of the Mouth Ritual

The Mouth Opening ceremony, an ancient Near Eastern ritual, consecrates statues with a divine presence.[30] Extant descriptions of the rite, mostly from eight-ninth centuries BCE Babylonia, are precious evidence of one view of how the consecrations worked. By contrast, Hebrew Scriptural texts attack the process. For practitioners, the rite of statue consecration was interpreted positively as

---

25 For a general discussion of the Deuteronomic source in the context of the documentary hypothesis, see Baden (2012, 129–148).

26 New meanings for a name dwelling in a place will develop in the first centuries CE as discussed in the next example.

27 The ideology permits many ideas about names. Hundley (2009) enumerates: name as legally binding, as marking a de facto owner, as obligating someone.

28 Hundley distinguishes between ancient naming and modern, oversimplifying the latter (2009, 549).

29 See above, page 31.

30 In addition to the bibliography cited here, see Suter (2012).

bringing about a divine presence, for critics it negatively demonstrated the inability of worshippers to understand the true nature of divinity. Given the use of all sorts of material representations just outlined of divinity by the Israelites, this debate is a rich opportunity to examine ideas about the materiality of signs and the divine presences the materiality represented.

No complete text of the Mouth Opening rite is extant, but numerous overlapping fragments illustrate the main stages.[31] The rite begins by asking the permission of the god and gathering the materials necessary for making a statue, leading to the consecration of the statue. The consecration mirrors the birthing process, with references to the spreading of semen, midwives, and the delivery of the statue through a wooden birth canal; all of this results in a statue "born in heaven."

The rite maps the arrival of a god's earthly manifestation and not the story of the birth of a god per se. The imagery of birth points to a very tight connection between the divinity and the statue, an idea that had a lasting impact on Israelite theology. The birth contains elements of familiar human birthing but is radically distinct. Perhaps most important, this representation insists on an intertwined iconic and indexical mode of sign representation that is hard to disentangle. The form of the statue is iconic of divinity and the specific consecrated birth process points to the divine status of a particular statue. The process is yet another version of a "baptismal event" that cements the connection between the god and that specific statue (a rhematic dicent). Much like the rigid representation of a divine name, the statue cannot easily be recontextualized to stand for something else. To speak in Durkheim's terms, it cannot easily be desacralized (Durkheim 2001, 77).

This consecration process contrasts with the ideology of production of Greek statues which were not consecrated as vessels or incarnations for divinity by a specific ritual (Steiner 2001, 114–120). Instead the divine presence might appear or disappear at will. The deity could abandon a statue as it might a house or any other place it chose to temporarily inhabit. A similar model is found in some biblical passages where the Temple is described as a house that the deity can inhabit or abandon.[32] The divine presence, for example, leaves the Temple in Ezekiel, a process described as moving out of one house for another abode (Ezekiel

---

31 For the ceremony, see Walker and Dick (1999) and Levtow (2008, 88–100). Most of the evidence comes from ninth- and eighth-century BCE Babylonia, except for some partial citations from the period of Gudea of Lagash (ca. 2150 BCE).

32 This transient imagery of divine presence suited the utopian model of the universe, as seen in Philo's claim that Moses did not settle into his body but merely took up temporary residence (*Confusion of Tongues* 77–82).

10:18 – 19). This is far from the only model. Other consecrated objects might be harder for the divinity to leave, as for example, the Ark of the Covenant.

The ritual distinguishes between the material the statue is made of and divine incarnation. The makers of statues describe the limitations of the mundane materials that they work with: the statue cannot smell incense, drink water, or eat food without the Opening of the Mouth (Dick 2005, 59)![33] Detailed attention is given to the process of making a lump of raw material into a divine vessel. Only those statues made according to the special rite and inspirited by the deity itself become divine receptacles. They are not simple productions of a human who builds an image: they result from a complex process requiring actions by both humans and gods.

Numerous strategies articulate the divine roles in fashioning—that is, how the object "pivots to the sacred" by nonhuman means (Gennep 1960). The gods are involved in selecting the workers, determining the site for the work and the time it will occur (Walker and Dick 1999, 115). Specific individuals may, for example, be told to make images (Hurowitz 2012, 274). All these determinants are signs that shift the intention and control of the process away from the human craftsmen and to the gods. The Opening of the Mouth was the moment at which the divinity took up residence in the statue.[34]

The statue maker did not believe that his actions brought the god into existence.[35] Nor did a statue displace a deity. As Michael Dick explains (1999, 33), "the Mesopotamians clearly maintained a distinction between the god and his/her statue." The destruction of a statue, therefore, did not signal the destruction of the deity. Stauer argues that statues of "everlasting wood" (the flesh of the gods) were destroyed as a sign that the gods were languishing without the requisite human attention (Schaudig 2012). Additionally, a deity's inability to protect his statues, his temples, and his people were all signs of the deity's weakness.

Access to divine statues was an opportunity to interact with a divine presence. Every mode of eradication reflected ideas about the original divinization of a cultic object. Destruction of statutes might be considered a humiliation of the deity or a return of the statue to the status of the materials out of which it was first made. The mouth and nose might be destroyed in an act of ritual-reversing (Woods 2012, 36). Statues were buried and decapitated (Woods 2012, 18, 36).

---

33 See also Walker and Dick (1999, 141).

34 This imagery compares with painting the eyes on statues in Hindu rituals (Winter 2000).

35 For a survey of satirical critiques of statues representing divinities, see among others Dick (1999, 31).

Sauer notes that specific modes of destruction were used in specific locales, as if ideas about proper destruction were very local (Sauer 2014, 24).[36]

Scriptural texts mock statue consecration in ways that became foundational to later debates.[37] Prophetic parodies carefully cite the consecration rites, repeating almost-identical phrases about the state of the materials before the consecration.[38] The prophetic editors adopt phrases about the statues' inability to smell or eat, reusing the shared phrases for their own polemical purposes. Everyone agrees, for example, that prior to a consecration ceremony, a statue is simply a lump of some type of material. This idea, included in the consecration rite, can be turned into attacks simply by leaving out the part of the rite where the divine spirit transforms the material (Hurowitz, 2012, 266–267). This partial citation turns the rite against itself, shifting a consecration into a critique. Each step of the consecration is criticized, as Hosea 8:4 emphasizes the role of the craftsmen, thus negating the role of the divinity.[39] Other texts imply incorrectly that the rite creates the deity: Isaiah 44:15 claims, "And he made a god and worshipped it; he constructed a cult statute and venerated it." Dick characterizes Isaiah's stance as "a conscious distortion forged in polemics" (Dick 1999, 45).[40] Due to their extensive citation, these critiques preserve, perhaps unwittingly, the sheer variety, and technical complexity, of the consecration rites (Dick, 1999).

A suggestive comparison for the Mouth Opening ceremony is Christian relics. It is often hard to know the sign status of a religious object because the object has no inherent sign status, as we saw in the variations of how statues were understood to represent divinity.[41] A statue might be interpreted as a general diagram or model for statues (a rhematic legisign). Or a statue might be singularly connected to divine presence. A Christian relic, for example, that represents something as inextricably connected to the deity as smoke is to fire. Even in these cases, particular discourses as well as ritual practices can be used to highlight and reinforce this interpretation. Relics will be handled in such a way as to clarify to the audience that these signs are inextricably connected to divinity de-

---

36 Current controversies about the destruction of statues are evidence of how important these processes are.

37 See Isa 40:19–20, 41:5–14, 44:6–22; Jer 10:1–16; Hos 13:2.

38 Levtow offers a detailed discussion of the rhetorical goal of these parodies, each of which "is a culturally local, sociopolitical act of classification, power and social formation" (2008, 42). See also Berlejung (1997) and Dick (1999).

39 See also Jer 2:27, 3:9, and Hab 2:18–19, discussed in Dick (1999, 41).

40 For a satirical critique of Yahweh as "an obscure desert god who liked to live in an acacia box" see Dick (1999, 45).

41 This point needs frequent repetition since it is so tempting to simply classify signs based on one set of sign meaning.

spite have a distinct materiality. Bones are a good example, since bones have such a clear indexical capacity, but relics can, and did, take many other forms. In all cases the need is to balance the "mere materiality" of its "presencing" effect (Parmentier 1997, 50). A copy could be treated ritually to give it a connection to divinity and the presentation of extra copies does not take away, but might instead increase, the "creative indexicality."

Finally, the Mouth Opening rite belies the claim that all images were once considered holy.[42] Extensive manipulation is needed to transform the material into a receptacle for divinity. Nor does it make sense to say that statues, for example, have performative force. The generalization mixes together all sorts of much more specific interpretive moves about the social meanings of statues.

Example 3: The Divine Body as Hand and the Divine Name as Form

The mid-third-century CE Dura-Europos synagogue is famous for its floor-to-ceiling paintings of biblical scenes.[43] The building was miraculously preserved when, during a war between Persia and Rome, it was filled with dirt to buttress the city walls. The dramatic paintings depict numerous biblical scenes and characters, including a woman wearing only a necklace taking Moses out of the bulrushes. The striking nature of the painting has sent researchers in many directions in search of possible models.[44] Similar paintings are found in other, contemporaneous religious sites at Dura, suggesting shared workshops and artisans (Fine 2005b).

In the Dura synagogue, signs offer four different representations of the deity, all rubbing shoulders within the single building. Each of these modes could be interpreted as implying the others are not proper, but their presence in the same sacred space belies this stance. The examples represent different ideas about deference lacquered on top of each other. They are happy proof that literary attempts to organize and regiment the place and role of imagery do not even begin to outline how imagery was used.

In the first example of divine representation, several panels include a large hand complete with distinct fingers reaching down into a scene from just beyond

---

42 The particular time frame for this claim varies. See Benjamin (1968) and Belting (1994).
43 For the earlier analysis, see Kraeling (1979) and Goodenough and Neusner (1988); and for more recent discussion and bibliography, see Fine (2005a) and Fine (2014, 101–121).
44 The suggested models vary widely. Weitzmann and Kessler, for instance, argue for a basis in illuminated manuscripts, though none have been found (Weitzmann and Kessler 1990).

the frame. The hand clearly belongs to the deity. Each hand both offers a formal representation of the deity (the shape of his hand) and at the same time indexes, points to, the unseen body of the deity. The hand, a sign of the deity as the source of divine agency, activates the scene like a performative verb phrase. This mode of presentation solves a semiotic problem: how to clarify the role of the deity in Scriptural stories in a nonverbal manner. Each hand signals "The Lord caused this to happen" in a visual parallel to the narrative reports of the deity's role in unfolding events.

In one frame the deity is responsible for the parting of the waters for the Israelites (Exodus 13:17–14:29). Simply showing the parted water might be ambiguous, so no doubt is left as to the source of the dramatic event. The hand also occurs in the depiction of the resurrection of the dry bones in Ezekiel 37. The heavenly hand is busy raising up human limbs indistinguishable from the divine limb except for their connection to a divine body outside the frame of the painting. Again, the potentially ambiguous source of a miracle is clarified with a dramatic hand literally reaching into the story from outside the frame. An etiquette system permits the depiction of the hand without any other limbs. The hand of the deity overlaps with the phrase "hand of God" that appears throughout the Scriptural texts, one mode functioning as an interpretation of the other.

In the second type of representation, other scenes point to the deity by presenting stories in which he is a central character whose presence is indexed by other means. No hand appears, for example in the scene where the Israelite king is being anointed. The king is the deity's chosen representative on earth, and the anointing of the king points to the role of the deity as one who chooses the king. An image directs attention toward something subject to restricted representation. A throne points to the absent deity presumed to sit upon it.[45] As discussed above, according to Tryggve Mettinger and Brian Schmidt this mode is aniconic iconism, the use of some images to point toward other implied imagery.[46]

In the Jerusalem Temple panel Aaron stands in front of the Temple gate. He is dressed in his holy robes with his name inscribed next to him in front of the Temple building, clarifying exactly who this priestly figure is.[47] No one can see inside the building, and Aaron has no implements in his hand. In this case the Temple cult is presented as the outside of a building, with only the founder of the priesthood and no functioning priests present and no active sacrificing taking place. The Temple had long since been destroyed when the painting was

---

45 Scriptural texts include numerous examples of thrones as indexes of one kind or another divine presence. See Exod 15:17, 17:16, 24:10, Deut 30:2, Ezek 1:26, Isa 6:1 and Ps 45:7.
46 See p. 53.
47 Many other scenes indirectly point to the deity, such as the anointing of the king.

made; it has retroactively been made into a façade where all the elements are portrayed but not as part of any active cult. Inside the "closed portal," as the Temple scene is called, is the divine presence. What goes on inside the Temple is concealed; this concealing is represented by a curtain that both hides and stands for the mysterious innermost part (the curtain that separates the inner sanctum). No blood flows in this panel, in yet another idealized presentation of the Temple cult.

A third divine representation is the empty Torah niche. These niches are presumed to have held a Torah scroll.[48] The niches are similar to those in which statues were placed and are somewhat awkward for holding a scroll. This parallel with cultic statue niches is based on more than just the outward appearance. The tablets of the Law are treated as parallels to statues already in Deuteronomy 10:1–5, when Moses is told to put them inside the Ark (van der Toorn 1997). The Torah scroll is treated as if it is a statue, dressed like a person and carried in a procession (Tigay 2013). Prayer takes place before the niche, directed toward the sacred scrolls, just as if it would have been before a statue. In the context of the Dura synagogue, the Torah scroll sanctifies the synagogue by its presence, again just as a statue would.[49]

The area just above the Torah niche is decorated with an arrangement of the elements from the story of the near-sacrifice of Isaac in Genesis 22 (back of man, knife, animal, etc.), These elements invoke the deity's presence at this major sacrifice. Similar to the decorations in mosaics, this vocabulary of signs is a sort of Morse code for sacrifice and all of the implications of the story of Abraham's obedience.

Fourth, another formal divine representation and common mode of invoking divine presence is liturgy. A liturgical fragment was found among the ruins of the Dura synagogue. The prayer includes a fascinating blessing formula with a previously unknown version of the divine name.[50] The fragment reads (following Fine's translation):[51]

[Fragment A] Blessed is X, king of the world/eternity
apportioned food, provided sustenance
sons of flesh cattle to …
created man to eat of …

---

48 On Torah niches, see Schenk (2010, 201). They differ from the later Torah shrines that include either doors or a curtain over the scroll.
49 As one of many comparative examples, in 1 Maccabees 3:48, consulting the Book of the Law is equated with consulting the likeness of a god (Tigay 2013, 327).
50 For discussion and bibliography, see Fine (2005a).
51 See Fine (2005a) and the bibliography cited there.

many bodies of …
to bless all cattle …
[Fragment B] pure [animals] to [eat?]
provide sustenance
small and large
all the animals of the field
… feed their young
and sing and bless.

The exact purpose for the prayer is not known; the imagery fits a blessing after meals, but other settings are also possible (Fine 2005a, 56–57). The phrasing is similar but not identical to the standard rabbinic blessing formula: "Blessed are you, Lord our God, king of the world."[52] The phrasing is evidence that the liturgical formulas have not yet been standardized on the basic rabbinic model. Two striking differences from that model are first, the use of an X shape and second, the lack of a direct second-person addressee, "you." As to the first difference, the Hebrew alphabet does not include a letter shaped like an X. The character used appears to be a Greek chi. In the context of the prayer it is a substitute for a divine name. This striking usage is evidence of taboos against some ways of writing the name.[53] A divine name could be used liturgically.[54] The X points to (indexes) the deity and also is a formal representation (an icon) of the elided nature of divinity, of the extent to which the divine name cannot be used in the way that other words can. An entire ideology is encoded in the X form, paralleling other means of using but not misusing the divine name.

For the second difference, the blessing is not addressed directly to the deity as in the standard rabbinic formulas "Blessed are you." Instead it parallels the earlier declarations of the blessed state of the deity and of people vis-à-vis the deity. This formulation is closer to the inscriptions discussed above.[55] The lack of an explicit indexical like "you" does not mean that there are no contextual linkages, only that they are differently construed. It does mean that the dialogical stance (me/us speaking directly to you) is lacking even as the divine presence is invoked by other means (such as a name).

Once again prayer takes place in a site sanctified by multimodal formal and indexical representations of the deity, including a range of imagery and the di-

---

52 Kimelman dates the emergence of the standard rabbinic formula to the mid-third century CE, close to the date of the Dura synagogue's destruction (Kimelman 2005).
53 As argued by Fine, who cites a similar usage in the seventh-century Munich palimpsest. (2005a, 52).
54 Later rabbinic rulings permit the liturgical use of the name in the presence of ten men.
55 See pages 54.

vine name. All these divine representations overlap in the synagogue, one jostling with another. Layering of distinct divine representations reinforces the sacredness of the space. In that specific context the hand serves as an interpretive guide to the other paintings that do not include a hand. Not writing down the deity's name, surrounding it with careful restrictions, casts a shadow over any direct replication of the name as heresy or magic. The deity is both present, expressed through mere materiality, and also at the same time, transcendent of that very materiality.

The Fashions of Imagery: Examples from Many Gods Traditions

Turning to modern scholarship on images, Moshe Halbertal and Avishai Margalit's *Idolatry* (1992) is among the most influential studies of permitted and forbidden images. Halbertal and Margalit expound on the philosophical necessities of monotheism in contrast to polytheism's "ontological pluralism" (Halbertal and Margalit 1992, 8).[56] The details of this argument vary, but monotheistic theology is understood to be inherently and unavoidably hostile to imagery.[57] Not only is that claim historically inaccurate, but it oversimplifies the issue of how and when imagery was permitted and championed in "many gods" traditions. This point must be addressed before looking at the other details of their theory of idolatry since it includes an overly-narrow conception of polytheism.

Two studies, one on Buddhist statues and another on the use of statues in Śiva worship, help shift the discussion away from generalizations about polytheism. These two examples focus on moments of change. Shifting attitudes toward images are tied to much more specific social conflicts and practices instead of generalizations about monotheistic or polytheistic beliefs. The first study focuses on Brahmanical views about images. As is often noted, Vedic texts center on elaborate sacrifices. Sacrifice texts assume that deities have bodies and refer to them, but the rites include no references to statues of the gods.[58] The emer-

---

56 Summarizing one strand of modern scholarship, Julien Ries argues in the *Encyclopedia of Religion* that rejection of idolatry is due to monotheism (Ries 1987, 73). Edward Curtis in the *Anchor Dictionary of the Bible* states that "Christianity had its origin out of a Judaism that had been purged of idolatry" (Curtis 1992, 380).
57 These arguments parallel the very popular stances that monotheistic traditions are more violent than polytheistic ones.
58 Again, this raises the question of any necessary philosophical connection between polytheism and specific forms of imagery.

gence of statues of the deities in the second and third centuries CE articulates with a shift to grand-scale temples (Davis 2001, 108–109). These temples were supported by a combination of wealthy patrons and religious specialists. The turn toward statues cannot be attributed to popular religion or practice. Instead some ritual specialists stood against other specialists, having a tug-of-war about what constitutes "tradition."

Some specialists sought to carry on the Vedic sacrificial practices. Others wanted to supplement or replace the worship of the gods with new liturgical practices thought to better convey central theological doctrines. The "theists" argued that a deity must be accessible for prayer in some concrete form. A post-Upanishadic text, the *Paramasaṃhita*, outlines liturgical practices with the claim that "God can be worshiped in embodied form only. There is no worship of one without manifest form" (Davis 2001, 113). Viṣṇu was known to incarnate himself in a fleshly body; so too he incarnated in stone (carved or unaltered). Insertions are added to texts such as an appendix on the care of statues. These additions are presented as if they simply elaborated the text.

Partly because of the tremendous influence of the philosophical ideas of *ahiṃsā* (non-harm), some Brahmans wanted to replace the animal sacrifices with grain substitutes. Other Brahmans wanted to replace the horse sacrifice with a new ritual cycle for Viṣṇu that takes place not on a Vedic altar constructed for the specific occasion but in an elaborate temple with statues of Viṣṇu. Liturgical changes accompanied rising and declining social roles for the various segments of the elite attached to the various rites. When the altar was abandoned, the Vedic priest was literally relegated to the end of the ritual line, given the role of holding a set of water pots (Davis 2001, 118–119).

It is only because of the rich extant evidence that we can trace these developments as part of a split in the Brahmanical classes. Distinct groups of elites differed about how to relate to the older sacrificial traditions. Where evidence behind the shifting rituals is missing, it is all too easy to turn to a premade explanation such as popular religion (Davis 2001, 115).

Some modern versions of Hinduism emphasize Vedic practices that do not center on statues.[59] This recovery of Vedic ideas was motivated in part by contemporary dialogues with European scholars whose visions of Hinduism associated statues with suspect sexual practices. In this context the move toward the use of divine statues, and the liturgies associated with them, was evidence of debased forms of religious practice. The images could then be seen as late addi-

---

59 See R. Davis's discussion of modern readings of Śaṅkara that emphasize his anti-image discourse (R. Davis 2001, 122–124).

tions and distortions that should be abandoned for the purer, and older, authentic, Vedic religious expressions.[60]

In the second study, on the rise of Buddha statues, Gregory Schopen argues that it was specifically Buddhist monks and nuns who paid for the very first statues of the Buddha (Schopen 1990). In the case of these early statues, since no preexisting model of the Buddha was known, it was necessary to draw on existing models: "[T]he standing Buddha image is really a replica of the earlier standing *yaksa* or royal image, but lacking the regalia and insignia of royalty" (Schopen 1990, 166). Despite this origin, these images became so standard that it is hard to imagine Buddhism without them.

Why was adapting the royal statuary into Buddhist temples so important for nuns and monks? The statues were often dedicated to the families left behind by the ascetics who joined the temple. Schopen argues that the renunciation of household life was fraught with difficulty, since these monks and nuns came primarily from Hindu families. As they turned to the life of the ascetic, they "sought the face of a fellow human being where an earlier generation had wished to see the simmering presence of a bodiless power" (Schopen 1990, 168).

Later Buddhist texts lose sight of this conflict as the social context of Buddhist beliefs changes. The role of nuns in setting up statues was completely forgotten as the nuns themselves were forgotten. The "bodiless power" in Buddhist philosophy remained a core theological tradition and was always there to be revived as part of practices that included Buddha statues.

These two studies demonstrate that the use of statues may appear in relation to a very specific locus of power or social context, even in the case of polytheism. That historical context may then pass, and the original impetus behind the practice is lost. The practice may continue, with or without a new interpretations.

Halbertal and Margalit on the Forbidden Sign

Returning to Halbertal and Margalit, they are well aware that biblical texts do not agree on the proper modes of worship. Nor do they prohibit all anthropomorphic representations. They emphasize certain themes—including metaphysical error, the necessity for pure monotheism, and improper worship of the deity—as philosophical underpinnings for a consistent theory of idolatry. What is forbidden is based generally on "the struggle against mistaken or inappropriate rep-

---

60 Davis notes that language often supplies the theory of representation, but he does not develop this idea (R. Davis 2001, 121).

resentations" (Halbertal and Margalit 1992, 48). This struggle is an attempt to define the term "idolatry," and as the authors realize, no one definition of mistaken representation will suffice. That is, since anthropomorphism per se is not a problem, distinctions between types of representation are needed. As a first step, Halbertal and Margalit note but pass quickly over one biblical model in which improper worship is depicted through the metaphor of adultery. This model is of little help to the authors since it flies in the face of claims about the tight relationship between monotheism and idolatry. Jealousy of anything that may look like the worship of another god implies the existence of other gods.[61]

Halbertal and Margalit turn to semiotics for terminology to explain their core argument, stating that the Hebrew Scriptures prohibit only what are considered Peircean icons. With this point they have begun to shift the debate about idolatry. Peirce, however, outlined a set of different relationships between object, sign, and interpretant, not simply a set of classifications (Parmentier 1994, 49). To repeat a point made earlier, for something to be a sign, it must be interpreted to have a specific set of relationships with both interpretant and object. The meaning of a sign can easily be changed as these relationships are imagined. When a mode of representation is attacked as (for example) idolatry, it is retrodetermined to be a mode of representation that is viewed negatively, with no concern as to whether those who employ the sign would agree with the assessment.

Halbertal and Margalit never fully develop their use of semiotic terms. They mix Peircean with other terms ("similarity," "metonymy"), confusing their argument (Halbertal and Margalit 1992, 48). Simply put, their combination of analytic terms is not robust enough to differentiate consistently between the different modes of representation.[62] For example, a cherub is permissible, they state, since it is not a part of God but only something associated with the deity (Halbertal and Margalit 1992). This claim does not clarify how the cherub is understood to function as a sign, since "signs associated with the deity" is a very ambiguous classification. Similarly they note that the biblical editor did not worry that the deity's hand would be thought of as a substitute for the deity. Yet according to their own criteria, the deity's hand can be construed as iconic and thus, in their system, forbidden. They also argue that since no one is sure of what the deity looks like, some images are permitted. Yet again, these guesses at representations may be iconic, so no clear criteria emerge.

An act, in their analysis, "performed on the icon becomes an act upon the god itself," although no sign "is" a god (Halbertal and Margalit 1992, 40); each

---

61 See Morton Smith's analysis of Yahweh as a jealous god (Smith, 1952).
62 They also tie these terms into problematic notions of monotheism.

sign represents a god in a different way. Finally they state, "When an image is understood to be the god and not a representation of the god, that is idolatry" (Halbertal and Margalit 1992, 42). If this is the claim, then once again we see that idolatry does not exist as an analytic category. No form of representation inherently is "understood to be the god," since every representation has to be interpreted as such in some particular way.

Richard Parmentier, from a more consistent Peircean viewpoint, clarifies Halbertal and Margalit's distinctions. They are arguing that certain types of "similarity-based representations," which include cultic statues, are frowned upon; some iconic claims are rejected. "Metonymic representations," which include items such as cherubim and chariots, are permissible; that is, indexical claims might be permitted because they only point to divinity. Finally, if something is interpreted as a symbol, that may be less controversial; symbols are "conventional representations" that "describe the deity in linguistic metaphors that involve the mediation of an 'idea' [symbols]" (Parmentier 2009, 143). These distinctions outline not abstract classification but strategies of interpretation. Claiming that other people's signs are certain types of formal icons is a stance some biblical critics want to charge others with (You think your god has a body like a human's!) and then use when helpful (people are made in the image of the deity). Parmentier points out, "some theological rationalizations tend to transform the first iconic type into the second indexical type to deflect the charge of idolatry" (Parmentier 2009, 143). No one completely negates icons, since rituals depend on the indexical icons of divine presence (even if that is the Name embodied in a text). These claims are all acts of interpretation, not descriptions of practices. A ritual practice can be shielded from criticism by giving it a new retrodetermination that makes no claim about the ultimate form of the deity but instead offers a pointing-to (indexical) or symbolic (arbitrary) relationship with divinity. "Other rationalizations argue that icons are really symbolically-conventional so whatever is permitted for language-based representations should also be permitted for images" (Parmentier 2009, 143).

Challenges Describing the Forbidden Sign

The problem is obvious. Treating a drawing, a building, a statue, or a name, or, it should be added, a group of people, as a formal representation of divinity may seem like an idolatrous move. The solution is less obvious. How can the charge of misusing a sign be adjudicated? How can a sign's divine representation be proven? As Webb Keane explains, "Such clashes are especially apparent in the history of religions, which can place the very existence of the sign's object in question and thus exert pressure on the construal of that sign's semiotic ground" (Keane 2018, 81).

Abstract strategies to organize proper/improper signs vary and none are entirely successful. One approach is to take a moment when these debates are lexicalized, that is, when a term is invented that appears to synthesize a debate. Such is the term "iconoclasm" which appeared to offer a window into organized attitudes toward imagery.[63] The current popularity of the term means it will be used in an anachronistic manner, clustering together diverse phenomena and obscuring the complex history of preservation of images (Bremmer 2008, 14 – 15).[64]

A second approach is to posit a particular historical setting as the site of a fundamental break with signs past representations (including divine representation). Hans Belting places a dramatic shift in attitudes toward images in eleventh-century ties to iconoclasm, resulting in a transformation of the holy relic into secular art (Belting 1994). All images were holy until that period, which saw the rise of non-religious art for the first time (Belting 1994). David Freedberg counters that images remained powerful (that is, continued to have indexical meanings) in subsequent periods while some art forms functioned as secular art long before Luther (Freedberg 1996).[65] Once again, there is no single history of divine signs or, in Peircean terms, no simple account of the shifting contextual implications of sign meaning.

A third solution is to look for a setting in which the regimenting of sign meaning is more explicitly done and to focus on that setting. Elsner, for example, champions "ritual-centered visuality" where ritual is the preferred frame for viewing (Elsner 2007, 16). This emphasis on ritual is an attempt to map the regimentation which the frame of ritual might be thought to offer.

In the past, semiotic arguments were settled by brute force. The Byzantine emperor Leo III used anti-imagery polemics to explain the Christians' defeat by the Arabs; the Christians had been using too many images in their liturgies and were now being punished (Olster 1994, 424). He consolidated control over

---

63 In addition to those cited below, see Ellenbogen and Tugendhaft (2011), Gamboni (1997), Freedberg (1985), and Brown (1982).

64 Bremmer finds that the first extant Greek usage (*eikonoklastes*) is in a letter written by Germanos, eunuch patriarch of Constantinople (early 720s) (Patrologia Graeca 98, 189b). The first English term appears in England around 1420 in the anti-image writings of John Wyclif (iconoclasta) while the term "iconoclasm" only appears in 1797 (Bremmer 2008, 7 – 13).

65 Leone and Parmentier argue that it is a mistake to characterize an epoch of history as the Axial Age based on whether they are presumed to be able to reflect on representation and images (Leone and Parmentier 2014, 57).

rivals in the Church who happened to employ images in their liturgical practices as he was trying to exploit the Arab victories to centralize his power. The particular historical circumstances that shaped his rule offered the opportunity to use that specific rhetoric because of the Arabs' stunning victories at the same time as church liturgies were employing icons. Here we see that as in the Brahmanical and Buddhist setting discussed above, the determination of sign interpretation was based on very local constraints and historically contingent alliances between religious groups and their liturgical and cultic practices.

The vital point is that signs are constantly being reinterpreted, so that how a specific sign stands for a deity is also open to constant revision. Anyone's symbol can be read by someone else as having an existential or formal dimension, opening up that sign for critique. Even a divine name can become an idolatrous iconic image, so the emphasis must be on the interpretive system to correct the reading of the sign. Attacks on religious practices are always undertaken while looking back over the shoulder at a prior meaning. No practitioners would claim that they worship wood, or stone, or words; yet from someone's point of view that is exactly what happens.

4 Late Antique and Modern Semiotic Models of Letter and Spirit

The slim word "spirit" is called upon to do heavy lifting in the study of Late Antique religions and of religion in general.[1] "Spirit," along with the process "spiritualize," is said to re-center a religion for the diaspora, trouble the academic categories religious and secular, and motivate ethical development in ancient religions.[2] The historical sweep of "spirit" is immense; claimed by some as the secret center available only to the few, references to spirit are used as if a straight line can be drawn with only a few minor zigzags from Paul's interpretation of circumcision to Burning Man rituals.

As a baseline definition, Francis Clooney (1985, 365) summarizes Robert Daly's influential formulation: "By spiritualization, Daly means the process by which the Scriptural authors gradually focus their attention on the interior requisites for proper sacrifice, instead of the material performance itself. While this did not signify an anti-materialistic prejudice (as was the case, perhaps, in certain schools of Greek thought), it did relocate the meaning of sacrifice as interior to the performer and not external" (Clooney 1985, 365). Aware that this definition sounds suspiciously like Christian theology, Clooney adds, "One need not be Christian to understand that the sacrifice 'from the heart' is preferable to that of burnt offerings, or that God is most pleased by service in the community" (1985, 365).

Contra this popular stance, Jonathan Klawans argues that is it "high time to abandon the term 'spiritual'" (2002, 13). No one views their own rituals as lacking a spiritual dimension (Klawans 2002, 12). Trying to flip the basic model, Klawans reconfigures prayer in terms of sacrifice and not the other way around. Instead of thinking of prayer as an improved form of ritual that replaces sacrifice, sacrifice is imaged as the organizing principle for understanding other rituals.

Klawans's critique of the use of "spiritual" is a major step forward, but his substitute mode of comparison remains vague. He does not offer a robust enough way of differentiating between types of representational meaning for either sacrifice or prayer. For example, Klawans posits that the Last Supper is a metaphor of sacrifice (2006, 221–222). This comparison lumps together diverse

---

1 "Spirit" is only one possible translation of the Greek *pneuma*, an issue discussed below in some detail.

2 On replacing the practice of animal sacrifice with the spirit of sacrifice central for diaspora Jews, see Lieber (2007, 204); on troubling the categories, see Huss (2014, 47–48); and on spiritualization as ethical development, see Stroumsa (2009).

https://doi.org/10.1515/9783110768602-005

"standing for" models of both sacrifice and the body/blood meal as well as leaving unanswered questions about how the various signs are understood to stand for divinity. Metaphors are a very vague of (pseudo)definition that attempt to explain something in terms of something else.[3] How these pseudodefinitions work is neither obvious nor predetermined; their meaning is part of the same complex and shifting sign interpretations already encountered. Sacrifice rituals are built on "standing for" relationships, as is prayer, so what is being compared are representations of representations.[4]

These ancient and modern comparisons, this chapter argues, were based on ancient idea about how words and other linguistic units function. The first section of this chapter analyzes Paul's linguistic-based model comparing "letter" with "spirit." This model not only associates positive qualities with certain entities but, more important, endows only some entities with symbolic representational capacity. The term "spiritual" is a word of attack and defense about modes of representation and offers a built-in polemical basis for how rituals are understood to fulfill or fail to fulfill religious goals. The second section examines a parallel discourse about "spiritualized" cult in Josephus and early Christian writers. The third section then looks at the limitations of modern recycling of the ancient spirit/letter hierarchy found in modern theories. A central concern throughout the sections is why "spirit" is such a Rorschach image, eliciting endless associations from ancient readers and modern writers.

Paul's Pseudodefinitions of Letter and Spirit

Theological doctrines are often built from small bits of linguistic ideology raised to the level of models for truth. Paul made one slice of Late Antique linguistic ideology famous when he hierarchically compared *gramma* (letter) and *pneuma* (spirit).[5] Paul is not the originator of this idea but its inclusion as a scriptural text turned it into an influential model for generations. The central challenge is not to fix a specific meaning for these two terms but instead to see what linguistic model determines the comparison and all subsequent uses of the comparison.

Paul employs this model in three passages:

1. "For a person is not a Jew who is one outwardly, nor is true circumcision something external and physical. Rather a person is a Jew who is one in-

---

3 See pp 1f. above.
4 See Hubert and Mauss (1899) and Valeri (1985, 77).
5 From the massive bibliography on Paul, only a few studies specific to the interests of this example are cited below.

wardly, and real circumcision is a matter of the heart—it is spiritual and not written" (Rom 2:28 – 29).[6]

2. "Our competence is from God, who has made us competent to be ministers of a new covenant, not of letter but of spirit; for the letter kills, but the spirit gives life" (2 Cor 3:5 – 6).[7]

3. "Now if the ministry of death, chiseled in letters on stone, came in glory so that the people of Israel could not gaze at Moses' face because of the glory of his face, a glory now set aside, how much more will the ministry to the spirit come in glory?" (2 Cor 3:7).[8]

Paul's concept of spirit is associated with a valid and important ritual, circumcision of the heart. This ritual in turn marks a true Jew. "Spirit" is explained as a type of linguistic unit—that is, a word. In Romans 10:8 he argues, "But what does it say? The word is near you, on your lips and in your heart (that is, the word of faith, which we preach)." In this case "word" is an interesting representational model; a word was imagined to be both something someone could say as part of a positive mode of speaking like preaching but also something that can be can associated with the heart. Paul employs two Greek terms, *logos* and *rhēma*. The association with lips is positive; even though it would be possible to imagine lips as lying, they are troped as uttering divine meanings.

Similarities and differences between spirit and letter do not exist inherently in these terms, as is true of any comparison (Goodman 1972). The basis of the comparison is stabilized by the modifiers associated with it and the way these modifiers are also nestled inside Paul's related but more frequently employed contrast between spirit and flesh. A letter is associated with flesh. This "flesh" letter has numerous negative associations since it kills and is connected with death. Letters, as flesh, are part of the lower world, which has limited connection to divinity. Spirit models all the best connotations that a linguistic unit can have.

This linguistic model is far from obvious. It is employed without any question of other possible relationships between linguistic forms. A written linguistic form may, for example, be understood as an exact copy of a spoken or oral form, or even as an improved version of a spoken word. The comparison's halves are

---

6 οὐ γὰρ ὁ ἐν τῷ φανερῷ Ἰουδαῖός ἐστιν, οὐδὲ ἡ ἐν τῷ φανερῷ ἐν σαρκὶ περιτομή· ἀλλ' ὁ ἐν τῷ κρυπτῷ Ἰουδαῖος, καὶ περιτομὴ καρδίας ἐν πνεύματι οὐ γράμματι.

7 ἀλλ' ἡ ἱκανότης ἡμῶν ἐκ τοῦ θεοῦ, ὃς καὶ ἱκάνωσεν ἡμᾶς διακόνους καινῆς διαθήκης, οὐ γράμματος ἀλλὰ πνεύματος, τὸ γὰρ γράμμα ἀποκτέννει, τὸ δὲ πνεῦμα ζῳοποιεῖ.

8 Εἰ δὲ ἡ διακονία τοῦ θανάτου ἐν γράμμασιν ἐντετυπωμένη λίθοις ἐγενήθη ἐν δόξῃ, ὥστε μὴ δύνασθαι ἀτενίσαι τοὺς υἱοὺς Ἰσραὴλ εἰς τὸ πρόσωπον Μωϋσέως διὰ τὴν δόξαν τοῦ προσώπου αὐτοῦ τὴν καταργουμένην.

also not equally weighted. One side is valued above the other in a hierarchy of prestige (J. Z. Smith 2004, 253). This hierarchical distinction is central to the use to which the comparison is put. The very arbitrariness of the hierarchy turns out not to be a problem but is instead essential to its efficacy.

The beauty of the linguistic contrast between "spirit" and "letter" is that it is incredibly flexible. This flexibility will become clearer as the linguistic basis of the hierarchical model is clarified. Generations of readers interpreted, expanded, and explained the contrast of "spirit" and "letter" in different directions. In these interpretations, the term "spirit" was defined by whatever concepts were considered the essence of Christian theology. Thus, the entry under "πνεῦμα" in the *Theological Dictionary of the New Testament* [Hermann Kleinknecht, *TDNT* 6:334 – 335] glosses as "not gramma but scripture self-attested through the spirit of Christ," which opens up endless possible interpretations. Contra this capacious understanding of the term, attempts are made to more narrowly define Paul's "spirit" by placing the term in various cultural contexts such as Stoic philosophy or Pneumatic medicine.[9] These attempts to pin down a specific meaning for "spirit" miss the heart of Paul's strategy, though they indirectly illuminate why any firm definition fails.

In contrast to these attempts to fix a stable meaning, Daniel Boyarin describes the distinction as a "metalinguistic practice."[10] Boyarin both opens and then, as we will see, forecloses this avenue of investigation. Specifically, when Paul talks about "spirit," Boyarin posits that Paul is engaging in allegory with the particular goal of "a search for unity" (1994). This is a complex metalinguistic process. For Paul's "flesh" side of the equation, however, Boyarin, searching for a stable definition for the "flesh" half of the contrast, posits a very specific non-allegorical view of the body. Paul's notion of flesh assumes a standard "Platonic dualism." Boyarin's new twist is that Paul does not completely denigrate the body.[11] Instead Paul's "flesh" presumes a scriptural pro-body stance dominant in at least some strands of Judaism.

Boyarin has in effect flipped the standard reading of the spirit/letter hierarchy by advocating for the "flesh" side. He elevates what usually occupies the lower rank in the hierarchy of comparison. This side aligns with modern values. It offers them a usable past and therefore deserves a second look. This reverse advocacy sustains the metalinguistic stance and uses it much as Paul did to con-

---

9 For the former, see Martin (2006) and for the latter, see Robertson (2014). For another version, the argument that the two terms refers to two "ways of life," see Principe (1983).

10 For his important critique of over-simple definitions of spirit see Boyarin (1994, 69).

11 He uses the term in a general way despite shifts in attitudes about materiality from Plato to his later interpreters.

struct a social evaluation. Boyarin preserves the hierarchy and its inherent evaluations but offers it in inverted form.

Boyarin has pointed us toward metalinguistics but has not explained the metalinguistic role of the letter/spirit comparison. The metalanguage noted by Boyarin is what linguists call "pseudodefinitions." As Silverstein writes about these comparisons, "Just such a definitional form is the perfect vehicle for *metaphorical pseudo-definition*, where we are not dealing with reference to specific objects seen as somehow similar, but with *pseudo-metasemantic equivalence* of conceptual categories" (1981, 4). The central task of the pseudodefinitions is not to organize the meaning of the words but to clarify the conceptual categories (fleshness vs spiritness). "Spirit" is understood to point to the life-giving divinity's connection with the individual via spirit. Letter outlines a different conceptual category (what kills).

The meaning of the terms turns out to be both more plastic and less important than the massive attempts made to narrowly define them in both the ancient world and modern scholarship. The importance of pseudodefinitions lies in their metapragmatic implications and these are far-reaching. As signs of the heart, anything equated with spirit can manifest and regiment intention (the intention of the heart and the meaning—or lack thereof—of an action). Anything equated with letter loses these capacities. This context-effecting linkage is the most important point about the dichotomy. In sum, Paul's claims are not about the denotational meaning of the terms "flesh" and "spirit," even including all the ways in which reference is played with in the models of allegory. Instead the importance of Paul's contrast lies in the metapragmatic entailments of the contrasting terms, defining how they can function as linguistic units.

It is vital to state clearly that the contrast functions both metasemantically and metapragmatically. In addition to presenting the pseudodefinitions which attract so much attention, it also outlines the context-effecting capacity of the linguistic terms in a way that is hidden from view. By (pseudo)definition, one half of the comparison has a different kind of standing-for relation with what it represents than the other part of the comparison. The "letter" cannot be interpreted allegorically or based on any other mode of characterizing a standing-for relationship; it can be understood only as a formal representation of materiality. The meaning of "spirit" *must* be interpreted allegorically; it can function only as a symbol that points to something in an arbitrary way. Everything from a ritual to a building can be evaluated based on this dichotomy. For example, Boyarin states, "from fleshly kinship to kinship according to promise and faith commitment, from earthly Jerusalem to heavenly Jerusalem, is certainly a move from the material to the spiritual." What type of linguistic unit the words are is the metapragmatic function of language. The unit "spirit" operates as a linguistic unit in a way completely other than "letter." What looks like a simple comparison, a metaphor, or an allegory, is carrying out a more complex linguistic task. "Spirit" is associated with a contextual implication of what spirit can do (give life). In contrast to the letter, the "spirit" word points to the lips and the heart (indexes them) and, even more astounding, has a formal relationship with them ("spirit" formally stands for life). Boyarin has captured only some parts of Paul's linguistic ideology, stating most directly, "spirit is the meaning for language prior to its expression in embodied speech" (1994, 16). This is a metapragmatic claim about the potential multifunctionality of parts of language and raises the question, why would these units be thought to work this way?

They are thought to work in this manner because that is the built-in linguistic model. In theory, the "earthly" Jerusalem could serve as an allegory; but that option is not possible by definition. Only some words and some social constructs can contain the dual "standing for" relationship necessary for a symbolic reading of that entity: "Since it is from the material expressed in material language to a set of ideas more abstract than the ones expressed by the material language, this is certainly allegorical, just as Paul would have it, and eloquent evidence for a dualist sensibility" (Boyarin 1994). Reversing and extending Paul's metalinguistics is an easy way to champion some versions of Jewish theology, since the contrast is so flexible and multivalent. As centuries of Christian theology have demonstrated, the contrast worked as a flexible guide for revitalizing any theological idea by connecting it to a positive symbolic meaning that can be spun out as needed.

The linguistic model that Paul adopts permits only one half of the equation to have a double representational status, to stand for something. The "flesh" part of the contrast has limited linguistic capacities because of the type of meaning that the term represents. Earthly Jerusalem has no representational value. It does not have any allegorical potential; it cannot stand for anything. It is simple materiality, like written language, which by definition can be only one half of a strict dualism that assigns allegorical potential to the other half.

Boyarin is aware of the limits of context-free definitions, which will not be able to settle all the issues he raises about the terms "spirit" and "flesh." That is, what these terms mean is not a simple issue of looking into a dictionary but instead involves figuring out their functions. The evidence refuses to settle neatly into any familiar parameters of definition, he correctly notes, even with his fine-tuned attempts. Given this situation, Boyarin argues that there are limits to how much the meaning of the terms can ultimately be specified. Their content —that is, their denotation—is in part contextual. If so, then we have located, though not yet made explicit, something central about the semiotic model that Paul is employing.

Furthering out metapragmatic investigation, claims about how words stand for what they represent are not the same for the two parts of the contrast. "Flesh" is understood to have meaning entirely based on the linguistic function of definition—and a narrow notion of definition, at that (it can be replaced by other literal equivalents, but that is it). Some words do not stand for anything beyond a simple notion of reference. "Spirit" on the other hand, and again by pseudodefinition, has to be interpreted in order to be understood. Paul does not explain this difference; it is assumed by his use of the contrast. "Spirit" and "flesh" turn out not only to have different meanings but to stand for those meanings in different ways.

What has Paul led us to take for granted? If "spirit" is equated with meaning, and "letter" with limited reference, the formal equivalency of "spirit" becomes the very act of finding meaning. The reference for "spirit" remains vague, any specific reference washed out. "Spirit" points toward any highly valued meaning, anything that has the form of heartfelt matters. Anything can be pointed to as "spirit" once it is equated with life-giving properties. "Spirit" can point to any heartful experience, as if talking directly about divine love without any other constraints on meaning.

Ironically, the referential content of the terms may vary over time, but the negative evaluation of letter/flesh remains stable. Any highly valued Christian theological belief is a commitment to spiritual meaning. In contrast, inferior theology is based on a commitment to a specific fleshly body of a person or a legal system or even a religious practice. Circumcision that is not circumcision of the heart has a formal relationship with death-killing signs; whether circumcision of the heart can occur along with actual circumcision is open to interpretation. Paul is pushing a pseudodefinition by which certain types of ritual are understood to implicate materiality, or the body, in ways in which other rituals are not.

Paul's model incorporates what are called "qualia": that is, evaluations associated with modes of speaking or linguistic units. Speakers "attribute sensuous qualities—e.g. lightness, dryness, straightness and others—to speech registers" (Gal 2013, 31). Qualia that may be associated with—index—something about, for example, a mode of speech are instead understood as telling us something formal about the speaker. What might have been seen as a mere convention (a co-occurrence) is now seen as conveying something about how things just are. Paul's qualia are dramatic, life-giving on the one hand, and connected to death on the other. These qualia shift from association with linguistic units like "letter" to other social registers, to actions and actors via pseudodefinition.

This linguistic-based model shifts unnoticed from one register to another in order to be of use in diverse cultural settings. Disparate parts of culture are understood to have the same standing-for dichotomy as "letter"/life-giving "spirit."

The model offers an instant hierarchy of representation that can be used to interpret many other levels, as in Gal's case about the qualia associated with different languages.[12] Only some rituals can be ethical, since only some are built with signs of intention.

"Letter" stands for the form of a ritual action (ethics not involved).
"Spirit" stands for the form of the actor's ethical intention.

Paul had his own distinct purposes for adopting and expanding this model. He uses it to set up a model for the reader in relation to his own writings. Paul's epistles are not *gramma* even if they may look to be, given that they are written. Instead they present matters of the heart that Paul conveys directly to the reader, as if bypassing their very status as epistles. The savvy reader will not be misled by the *gramma* but will go straight to the essential meaning of Paul's message.

The specific content of this contrast can be elaborated as needed in different historical settings, as is seen in the complex historical uses of "spirit". The term "spirit" is free to point toward a wide range of meanings provided that those can be interpreted to have the form of an abstract, positive meaning. This shift is indeed how the comparison will be used over the centuries, not as a term of reference but as a mode of relating form and meaning and putting them into a hierarchy. The contrast includes ideas about how "responsibility and intentionality are assigned to speakers in different cultural contexts" (Gal 1998, 424).

Idealizing Cult as a Rhetorical Strategy

In the same period another highly influential model for championing some rituals was being drafted by Josephus in his voluminous writings about Jewish practices and history.[13] Given the rethinking of the role of images in ancient Israelite cult discussed in the previous chapter, the role of images in Second Temple practices warrants close attention.[14] Josephus makes the first now-extant claim in a Jewish text that the Holy of Holies, the innermost part of the Temple, was entirely empty except for a curtain (Niehr 1997, 94). He thereby presents an idealized image of the cult that shares a nostalgic stance with many other Greco-

---

12 Gal cites Terry Eagleton's comment that "[S]uccessful ideologies routinely render their view of the world 'natural,' 'essential,' 'universal,' 'ahistorical,' and 'common sensical'" (1998, 429).
13 From the vast bibliography on Josephus, on this specific issue see Ehrenkrook (2008 and 2011).
14 See pages 31.

Roman texts.[15] A major impetus for presenting a totally-reformed cult came from an emphasis within the general culture, nostalgic in tone, that once upon a time, a pure, aniconic cult lay at the foundation of all subsequent religious practice.

In *The Jewish War* Josephus writes, "The innermost recess measured twenty cubits, and was screened in like manner from the outer portion by a veil. In this stood nothing whatever: unapproachable, inviolable, invisible to all, it was called the Holy of Holy" (*Jewish War* 5.219).[16] This description was written after the destruction of the building, an ode to the grandeur and mystery of the past. The three privatives, "unapproachable," "inviolable," and "invisible," are in sharp contrast to the reality; the Temple was entered by Romans and was then destroyed by them. In contradiction to the messy descriptions of the Temple during the revolt, Josephus impressed upon the reader that the Romans realized just how holy the building was even as they destroyed it. In Josephus's view the Romans recognized this sanctity better than the Jews who profaned the Temple. Statements about the lack of images in worship resonated with existing critiques in the surrounding culture, especially as they circulated among philosophically astute audiences. That is, even though the use of statues was widespread, many writers saw this as a debased practice.

Jason von Ehrenkrook argues that Josephus presented Jewish practices as more anti-iconic than they were in order to show that they demonstrate "true Romanness," creating a superiority shared by Jews and Romans over against Greek religious practices (Ehrenkrook 2011, 138).[17] This stance however, was not simply anti-Greek (Janowitz 2008). Greek culture also had a strong theme of anti-imagery found scattered throughout philosophical texts.

This view gave the Jews a theology that they could parade to non-Jews. They could unite behind it as both a moment of political rejection of intrusive control by outsiders (putting the image of the emperor in their place of worship) and as an opportunity to flaunt a belief that was widely shared.

---

15 This discourse is distinct from the entextualization of sacrifice traditions, where sacrificial rites are turned into segmentable textual units that talk *about* sacrifice (discussed in the next chapter).

16 Josephus describes the Temple elsewhere in his writings. See, for example, the extended symbolism discussed in *Jewish Antiquities* 3.180 – 187. Jason von Ehrenkrook notes that Josephus is not consistent is his descriptions of the Temple (Ehrenkrook 2011, 105). Josephus, for example, mentions carvings on the Temple ceiling (*Jewish Antiquities* 15.414 – 416) but elsewhere states that the Temple had no images but a coffered cedar ceiling (*Jewish War* 5.190 – 191).

17 Ehrenkrook, echoing Steven Weitzman (2005, 6 – 9), argues that Jews adopted contemporary themes for the purpose of survival. Whether the adoption of a common contemporary theme is for the purpose of subversion or to embrace some aspect of contemporary culture is very hard to tell.

Josephus and early Christian authors drew on Greek and Roman critiques of imagery, adopting their idealized depiction of aniconic religious practices. Despite the potential problem of touting a Jewish claim, and a claim that might be in conflict with Christian ritual practices, many early Christian texts reference superior aniconic practices. Authors hunted for and repeated any Greco-Roman writers who described image-free cults, no matter how fanciful the claims. These ideas are located in often quite ancient texts that were pillaged based on first-centuries CE concerns. A striking range of writers praised an idealized, aniconic ancient mode of religious worship. We have lost the contexts of these quotations and are not making any arguments about the use of these themes in their original contexts. Their importance here is their circulation in the first centuries CE in Christian writings. Clement (*Miscellanies* 5.14) cites Xenophanes's classic critique that the greatest god is unlike mortals in form and mind. Xenophanes mocked the entire question of the form gods are imagined to have, pointing out that if cows imagined the form of their gods they would think they looked like cows (Steiner 2001, 89 – 90).[18] Origen (*Cels.* 7.62) cites Heraclitus's rejection of offering prayers to images as part of a philosophical rejection of their efficacy: "And they pray to these images just as if one were to have conversation with houses, having no idea of the nature of gods and heroes." This critique of images is even more severe than Xenophanes's, since it ridicules prayer as well (Steiner 2001, 121). Origen (*Cels.* 1.5) also cites Zeno of Citium, the founder of Stoicism, who argued that there was no need for temples, since the work of builders and artisans should not be considered sacred. This stance is a more broadly-based rejection of traditional religion than the Israelite anti-imagery discourse. Antisthenes, preserved by Clement (*Miscellanies* 5.14), stated that knowledge of the deity cannot come from an image.

Early Roman religious practices included the use of both small statues in family rituals and larger statues in public cults. However, early practices were remembered as having no role for statues (Varro apud Augustine, *De Civ. Dei* 4.31). Plutarch (*Numa* 7.7) claimed that Numa forbade the Romans to "revere an image of God that has the form of man or beast." It was "impious to liken the higher things to lower, and ... it was impossible to apprehend Deity except by the intellect" (Plut. *Numa* 7.8). The earliest Greek religion was also remembered as being free of images. For example, Pausanias wrote (4.22.1), "At a more remote period all the Greeks alike worshipped uncarved stone instead of images of the gods."

---

18 See also Clement, *Miscellanies* 7.22.

Of particular interest to our discussion, foreign practices were in particular praised as being aniconic. These practices appeared to offer a good stick with which to beat local traditions: being exotic, they offered some special insight into grander religiosity. The Persians, according to Herodotus, did not believe that the gods have the same nature as men and therefore rejected building images, altars, and temples (*Hist.* 1.131). So too the Scythians used only a scimitar of iron as their image of Ares (*Hist.* 4.62). Strabo depicted the rejection of statues as one of the many sensible traits of the Nabateans (*Geogr.* 24.4.26).

Jewish modes of worship were positively evaluated based on this broad stereotype, much as Jews were praised for being philosophers whether or not that is the most accurate description. Strabo, for example, presented Moses as specifically rejecting the mistaken Egyptian representation of deities as beasts and cattle. He adds as a side note that the Greeks were also wrong in "modeling gods in human form" and that it would be better to make a sacred precinct without an image (*Geogr.* 16.2.35). Varro presents the Jews as persevering in their anti-iconic stance and not lapsing into error, unlike the Romans (Varro apud Augustine, *City Of God* 4.31).[19]

Even as anti-Jewish themes emerge in these writers, a philo-Jewish stance recognizes Jews as embodying an ideal not met by the author's own culture. In all such cases, looking outward to "barbarians" was a way of chastising and critiquing native practices. An idealized notion of Jewish theology was used as a measure for finding out just how far native practice had fallen from a golden aniconic past. Being known for the use of images in worship would have equated Jews with Egyptians, whom both the Romans and the Jews looked down on (Bohak 2003). Educated people would recognize that Jewish worship, unlike Egyptian religion, was based on a philosophy common to contemporary elites.

The aniconic description idealizes the Temple cult, continuing themes from Chapter One such as the non-human basis of cult. Sometimes the idealization presents the sacrificial cult in a perfected form, far from any realities of actual practice. *The Letter of Aristeas* presents a neverland of sacrifice where priests choreograph their comings and goings to avoid contact. These textual versions of Temple cult are powerful filters not only for whatever activities the daily running of the Temple included, but also for the chaotic depiction of Jewish factions fighting inside the Temple as part of the revolt. Stressing the purity of the cult permitted Josephus to use a Roman mode of argumentation against the Romans. Josephus, as part of his general advocacy, has to appeal to the superior stand-

---

19 See also Tacitus, *Hist.* 5.5.

ards of his readers. Josephus strove to make Jewish practices meet the international standard: that is, the standard of educated elite readers whom he saw
as sharing his worldview.

Josephus presents the empty *place* where cult is carried out as the ultimate
sign for transcendence. The entire cultic practice is regimented by this sign, as if
the building was only an index pointing toward the mysterious, distant deity. Josephus's idealized cult demands the highest moral standards and locates the
sacrificial cult as far as possible from the center of his religion.

Letter and Spirit in the Modern Study of Ritual

Shifted to the level of abstract theory, the pseudodefinition ideology that pits the
empty form of letter against a meaningful "spirit" word influences the modern
framework for comparing ancient religions. The framework forces religious actions with dense interpretations into a neat teleological model that points toward
Christianity. The model is used to explain the shift from animal sacrifice (letter)
to prayer (spirit), a story of religious displacement central to understanding Late
Antique religion.

In his elegant version, Guy Stroumsa (2009) contrasts Christian, Jewish, and
Greco-Roman religions by means of the linguistic "letter"/"spirit" model.
Stroumsa outlines "the main vectors of the radical and multifaceted transformation of religion" that occurred in the third century CE as Judaism outstripped
pagan morality and then in turn was outstripped by Christianity" (2009, xvi).
Stroumsa employs Paul's linguistic "spirit"/"letter" model in three specific arguments: (1) rabbinic sages reject a too-literal reading of sacrifice, following Paul's
model, but ultimately "reject metaphors" and embrace law (choosing letter over
spirit); (2) again equating abstraction with only some linguistic forms, an internalized word—a thought—is presented as the highest form of religious expression, since it is farthest from the *ex opere operato* rite of sacrifice; and (3) the
complete spiritualization of sacrifice could occur only with the destruction of
the Temple since the literal building (letter) inhibited allegorical thinking and
hence more interior meanings (spirit) for Jewish practice.

On the first point, Stroumsa quotes an oft-repeated saying attributed to
Rabbi Eleazer ben Pedat: "To do charity and justice is more acceptable to the
Lord than sacrifice. Prayer is higher than sacrifice" (bBer. 32b).[20] Stroumsa states

---

20 Cited at Stroumsa (2009, 68). Interpretations of the statement abound, some viewing it as an

that this saying proves that for at least some Jews, "alongside the blood of sacrifices, there is thus another sort of sacrifice that is spiritual" (2009, 61). We are back again to the concerns raised by Jonathan Klawans and the problem of claiming that some rituals are spiritual but others are not. Hubert and Mauss ended that argument when they outlined the complex ways in which the elements of sacrifice have a representational meaning (1899). Sacrifice has an inherently "spiritual" function for those who interpret it in this manner, which is indeed what happens throughout the history of Judaism.

In a great deal of modern analysis, the "spirit" dimension of the hierarchy is troped onto individual experience. It is impossible to question someone's experience, so experiences now supply the indexical (pointing-to) signs of religious truths.[21] Supplanting the more limited role that sacrifice can fulfill, a "mystical experience" can bring "an alliance between the community and its god(s)" (Stroumsa 2009, 58).[22] In addition to raising all the problems associated with claims of mystical experience, this statement negates the communal role envisioned for sacrifice.[23]

Troping directly off Paul's implied metapragmatics, Stroumsa argues that "The new religious status of the word gives it a power of action: to say is now to do, to use the title of a classic of modern philosophy, John Austin's *How To Do Things with Words*" (2009, 62–63). The spiritual "word" once again represents all metapragmatics rolled into one. Any ritual action is understood to be materially based, having by definition limited efficacy since it is a doing-in-itself.

Like Boyarin, Stroumsa sees this as a partial but ultimately unsuccessful Hellenization of the Jews.[24] Despite the stance of Pedat, the rabbis continued to invest ritual energy in nonspiritual actions, thus limiting the ethical potential the Jews had discovered in their flirtation with rites that more directly represented internal states. Their insistence on still carrying out nonspiritual rites limited their spiritualizing tendency and ethical potential.[25]

---

historical response to the destruction of the Temple; others, as part of a universal move away from animal sacrifice.

21 Thus the great interest in some possible neurological basis for religious experience that may lead researchers to the God gene, another possible modern model for truth.

22 This reverses the stance about sacrifice of an earlier generation of scholars who saw the communal meal as a close encounter with a deity.

23 Sacrifice as a communal experience figures in the writings of too many scholars to cite, including Robertson Smith and Emile Durkheim.

24 For this comparison to work, "Hellenism" is defined as certain strands of Platonic thought, and "Jewish" must be equated with biblical ideas.

25 The rabbis did contribute to turning sacrifice from deeds into words, since they were part of how "this transformation stressed the story of sacrifice. ... Ritual was transformed into the story

Not surprisingly, the ultimate spiritualization of religion is accomplished by Christian theology.[26] This spiritualization led to a new notion of self, necessary for the importance of religious experience and ethical thought. "The new care of the self cannot ignore ethics and intersubjectivity" (Stroumsa 2009, 25). Early Christian writers used this new care of the self to vanquish the Gnostic temptation. The heretical Gnostic movement is again an even more misguided (linguistic) ideology, taking some ideas too literally (evil) and others not literally enough (their attempt to liberate themselves from all constraints). Against this stance, normative Christian writers carved out the correct use of words, which permitted the development of more extensive moral meanings.

In Stroumsa's second use of the "letter"/"spirit" model, in brief, words are as far away as possible from the *ex opere operato* rite of sacrifice. They do not have to be said aloud but merely thought. An internalized word—a thought that has shed its "letter" form—is the highest form of religious expression. Stroumsa summarizes this stance, which explicates the negative, utopian view of body (troped as "letter") as, "Now it is the individual consciousness that is charged with constantly reinvigorating the relation with the divine. ... Ideally speaking, prayer and fasting, and charity are all practiced in silence and in secret" (2009, 69). Entire religions are associated with the literal, not just some forms of Jewish religious expression, as Stroumsa states: "Neither imperial religion nor mystery cults could conceive of the transformation of interior life and of rational discipline —this is found only among the philosophers and the Jews" (2009, 12).[27]

Finally, a third point Stroumsa raises is that successful metaphorization of sacrifices could take place only after the Temple was destroyed. As long as the Temple stood, it was impossible for certain types of discourse about ritual to take place: "In effect, it is only in a situation in which the sacrifice offered in the Temple no longer exists that such a metaphoric acceptance of the term might be developed" (Stroumsa 2009, 75). Certain types of allegorical readings of rituals can take place only under some circumstances, when any possible literal mooring is cut off by historical circumstances. Only with the destruction of the Temple will the rabbis and other Jews be able to replace sacrifice with an intentional mode of ritual: "Destruction of the Temple permitted the spiritualiza-

---

of ritual—into a myth, in a way" (Stroumsa 2009, 67). When a story is told about a ritual, it does not mean that all ritual is over.

26 For a similar and equally questionable evolutionary schema for notions of sin, see Anderson (2009). After a careful analysis of the terms used for sin, he ranks some terms as having greater ethical saliency for no apparent reason other than Christian theological concerns.

27 This view could be critiqued by finding equally spiritual claims made by Greco-Roman writers, but that does not help explain the grounds on which these theological debates took place.

tion of the liturgy, *leitourgia*, by transforming rites accompanying sacrificial activity, by prayers replacing the daily sacrifices, and by giving ancient prayers a value that they had not previously had" (Stroumsa 2009, 64).

Stroumsa is correct that Temples were replaced and Late Antique religions were outlined by the many ideas about replacement. This schema, however, lacks any theoretical explanation for the claim that Jews were not able to replace the Temple cult while the Temple stood. In addition, the Temple had to stand for something while it stood, and what the Temple represented was open to debate whether or not the Temple was standing. What was important was the religious imagination of the role of a Temple; in the terms of Jonathan Z. Smith, both how a Temple became a place and then how it was replaced (J. Z. Smith 1987b).[28]

Most distressing is Stroumsa's connection of ethics and morality with specific theological versions of linguistic ideologies. Interest in the Law (the written form—letters—minus the essential meaning of words) limited the Jews from following through on the ethical stance of the prophet. The prophetic ethical stance separated the Jews from the even greater lack of interest in ethics found in paganism since pagan thinkers were never concerned with community but only with individuals. Ancient Christians were able to move past the prophet on to the saint (Stroumsa 2009, 16). In this schema, the saint is a more ethical version of the prophet, since the saint literally acts out ethical beliefs whereas prophets just talk about them (appearing to reverse the evaluation of literal and metaphorical), leaving the prophet too abstract for a fully ethical life (railing against injustice but not dying for such a belief). Even if this is a direct extension of the linguistic model, instead of leading us to a superior way of analyzing ethics it demonstrates the basic problem with the entire approach.

One final example demonstrates the amazing flexibility of the hierarchical cultural "spiritualization" comparison, used in this case to argue for the superiority of Judaism. Sigmund Freud's analysis articulates yet another possible exploitation of the aniconic ideology from the last chapter combined with the letter/spirit model. He prefigures much current discussion about monotheism, if in ways that might make some monotheism enthusiasts uncomfortable.[29] Freud located the impetus for Jewish notions of idolatry in Moses's attempt to revive the fading monotheistic stance of the dead pharaoh Akhenaton. This monotheistic stance included a new attitude toward the deity, who is described in abstract

---

28 The Late Antique shift away from Temple and toward the figure of a Saved Savior is traced in Brown's classic article (1971).

29 His argument is found primarily in *Moses and Monotheism* (Freud 1953–1966 [1939], 23:7–137).

terms.[30] This abstract conception of the deity could not be expressed in imagery. Monotheism, the argument goes, is much more challenging for followers than polytheism. The theology also includes a strict set of ethical guidelines, again lacking in polytheism.

But if this prohibition [against images] were accepted, it must have a profound effect. For it meant that a sensory perception was given second place to what may be called an abstract idea—a triumph of intellectuality over sensuality or, strictly speaking, an instinctual renunciation, with all its necessary psychological consequences. (Freud 1953–1966 [1939], 23:113)

The instinctual renunciation and increase in intellectuality led to an increase in pride; hence the Jews' vision of themselves as the Chosen People.[31] This self-understanding is one of the reasons for the long history of the hatred of the Jews. Their rejection of sensuality stood as a refutation of everyone else's beliefs and thus elicited envy and scorn.

In his view the strict Jewish rules gave Jews an impetus to set themselves apart as the Chosen People. Since they challenged norms, they were the object of social stigma. The Jews represent an ancient tradition, the very best the entire ancient world (including Egypt) had to offer. The minority status of their views is due to their advanced views. Their ancient ideas were precursors of high-level moral thought that would not develop in other cultures for thousands of years (if ever). The Jews were the intellectuals of the ancient world, giving up the world of the body for the world of the mind. As for Josephus, Jewish rejection of imagery was the source of Jewish pride and the adulation of elites, even if it was misunderstood by many.

Discussing these claims, Peter Schäfer finds it ironic that the next level of hierarchical adjustment is when psychoanalysis triumphs over Judaism (Schäfer 2002, 395). This substitution is easy since the next level of spiritualization is always around the corner. Schäfer implies that even more ironic is that Freud's "triumph of spirituality" is born out of the spirit of Christianity (Schäfer 2002, 406). As we have seen, this linguistic model has no single birth and just as Boyarin can reverse the spirit/letter model to champion what he sees as a positive "letter" role for some Jewish ideas about the body, the spirit/letter model does not belong to any specific tradition. That Freud would claim the culmination of this tradition for Judaism points to his subtle understanding of the inter-religious tensions of this hierarchy and his willingness to reverse the model to what he sees as the benefit of Judaism. The rise of psychoanalysis in turn outdates Ju-

---

30 Negating the many narrative and nonabstract depictions in Hebrew Scriptures.
31 This claim distorts the role of every ancient group as chosen in relation to its deity.

daism as it is unmasked as one among many illusions. Ultimately the model permits to explain what most interested him, that is, it helped Freud as a Viennese Jew understand the persistence and power of anti-Semitism.

Freud's formulation, like so many reformulations currently being offered, is helpful neither as an historical explanation for the development of ancient ideas about aniconic monotheism nor as a general proof that people who use divine images have lower ethical standards.[32] The close tie between monotheism and either ethics or aniconic religious practices is a myth of monotheistic theology only slightly reformulated from ancient polemics. Worshipping one god, not many, becomes a metaphor for constraint in one form or another as an historically contingent rhetorical stance is raised to the level of an abstract philosophy. This is no surprise, since idolatry is a theological term that, once untied from the theology, does not sustain any specific psychological or philosophical coherence.

Spiritualization is a claim about representation based on what we can call a "folk understanding" of the meaning of words and action. In the ancient version, to call upon "spirit" was an act of interpretation based on a very specific ideology that implied how signs stand for thought and action: some words stand for divinity better than others. The claim to represent "spirit" was, and still is, a decoy that permits a shift from one cultural register to another and associates intentionality with a specific kind of action. The power of this linguistic model is proven by its longevity.

---

32 In the terms of Robert Paul, who rescues Freud from his own argument, the story of the horde Freud told was a thinly disguised version of the Torah story (Paul 1996). The story of Moses' rebellion against his adoptive father was not about what happened, but as with any myth, it motivated the social and religious institutions including the atonement sacrifices.

5 A Semiotic Approach to Ascent Liturgies

This chapter contrasts two liturgies that are part of ascent rituals, that is, trips to and through the heavenly realms.[1] The first, *Songs of the Sabbath Sacrifice*, comprises thirteen liturgical compositions found in numerous fragments at Qumran and also at Masada.[2] These compositions describe an ornate heavenly cult, detailing the ranks of angelic priests, their thrones, and the heavenly decorations and architecture. The second, *Ma'aseh Merkavah*, is part of the complex and hard-to-date "*hekhalot*/palace" corpus (third through eighth century CE) and also outlines the heavenly realm and describes angelic praise.[3] The textual history of these compositions is hotly debated.[4] As more detailed textual histories are being produced, it is valuable to examine some of their ritual strategies.

What Is an Ascent Ritual?

In the ancient cosmology often referred to as "locative," a simple trip up a mountain sufficed for Moses to join the deity for a meal (Exod 24:9–10a).[5] The trip is described in one sentence: Moses and Aaron, Nadav and Avihu, and seventy elders ascended and they saw God (Ex 24:9). The trip did not involve complex ritual actions or dense descriptions of the cosmos. Instead the short anecdote shows an ease for a close meeting with the deity that discomforts modern readers.

In later texts (beginning second century BCE), trips to heaven reflect a "utopian" multilayered heavenly world that is difficult to diagram.[6] A similar cosmic complexity appears in rabbinic texts that layer ancient ideas about the sandwich

---

1 In addition to the specific bibliography cited below, for a range of descriptions of ascent, see Himmelfarb (1993) and Johnston (1997).
2 The Qumran copies are written in generally datable Hasmonean (75–50 BCE) and early Herodian (25 BCE) scripts. For the critical edition, see Newsom (1985); for Cave Four see DJD 11, with important emendations in Tigchelaar (1998); and for Cave 11, see García Martinez, Tigchelaar, and Woude (1998) (DJD 23: 259–304). For translations and analysis, see Davila (2000); Fletcher-Louis (2002, 252–394); Alexander (2006); and the citations below.
3 For the Hebrew texts, see Schäfer, Schlüter, and Mutius (1981); for translations, see Davila (2013); and for discussion and further bibliography, see Boustan, Himmelfarb, and Schäfer (2013). On the contested relationship of these text circles to those that produced the normative rabbinic literature, see Vidas (2013).
4 See Schäfer (1988), Davila (1993), and Mizrachi (2009).
5 For the locative/utopian cosmologies see Smith (1978, 100–103, 13–42, 147–151, 160–166, 167–171, 185–189, 291–294, 308–309).
6 For the a summarizing contrast between locative and utopian see Smith (2004, 15–16).

https://doi.org/10.1515/9783110768602-006

heaven/earth (locative) model on top of or inside multilayered heavens that encircle the earth (utopian).[7] It is in this multi-layered cosmology that ascent rituals emerge.

The issue of ascent as a realizable ritual goal was unsettled by Gershom Scholem's insistence that ascent rituals found in the Hekhalot corpus were not a late medieval degeneration of rabbinic Judaism (Scholem 1960). Instead of being a late medieval invention, the corpus includes earlier material as do the more standard rabbinic texts. Scholem argued that ascent was a foretaste of the heavenly world (1965, 17–18). As we will see, ascent is a flexible ritual model that can be used for all sorts of ends.

No consensus has emerged about the techniques that undergird ascent rituals. Explanations include a very broad anthropological model such as Arnold van Gennep's rites of passage or a universal notion of a mystical, or shamanic trance.[8] These models are far too general and can be applied to almost any ritual.[9] Scholars seem flummoxed by a dearth of direct instructions that explain how an ascent rite works. About the *Songs*, Davila (2000, 93) states, "The *Songs of the Sabbath Sacrifice* contains no such instructions and presents the tour of the heavenly realm without making clear how it is being experienced. ... [M]agic and theurgy are entirely missing." Liturgical texts do not always include instructions such as "Do X in order to achieve Y." Happily, liturgy does include the high degree of self-reflexivity connected to performance (Bauman and Briggs 1990, 73).[10] This self-reflexivity offers a vital window on perceived efficacy even if it is not cast as explicit primary performatives of the Austinian type.

Liturgy is highly context-creating, invoking the presence of a deity or transforming a place from profane to sacred. Because it so obviously attributes power to words, liturgy is a vivid example of "the central place [language] occupies in the social construction of reality" (Bauman and Briggs 1990, 60). This reality includes other-worldly realms presupposed in a ritual. The issue with ascent rit-

---

7 See the attempts to draw several versions of the rabbinic cosmology combining old and new elements in Leicht (2013).

8 For the use of Van Gennep, see Meerson (2013). Alexander (2006, 8) cites the universal model of "the numinous experience" as outlined by Rudolph Otto.

9 For trances, see for example Schäfer's shaky distinctions between types of trance (1992, 154–155). For a counter to universalized claims about shamanic trance such as the one made by Davila (2001), see the helpful critique in Kehoe (2000).

10 Performance provides a frame that invites critical reflection on communicative processes (Bauman and Briggs 1990, 60). Alexander joins Fletcher-Louis in comparing the *Songs* to play scripts, which seems to undercut any need for extensive supplementary techniques (2006, 111).

uals is thus not so much a set of explicit instructions as the capacity of liturgical texts to create their own contexts of use, whatever those contexts might be.

More specifically, liturgies are effective because of all sorts of contextual linkages. These run from the more familiar performative words and phrases as discussed in Chapter Two to the poetic function of language. That is, the efficacy of liturgy is based on two quite distinct ends of the performative spectrum: specific formulas such as the "speech act" at one end of the efficacy spectrum and the poetic functions of language at the other (larger structural organization of liturgical texts).

In other words, self-reflexive verbs and ritual structure are both vital. The former's efficacy is more obvious to users and those who analyze rituals, being closer to primary performatives (and thus already discussed at some length). Less obvious but equally important is the latter, the poetic function of language. This function needs some unpacking. To bring greater precision to discussions of the multifunctionality of language, Roman Jakobson outlined six distinct functions (emotive, conative, metalinguistic, poetic, referential, phatic).[11] The poetic function is particularly central to poetry, hence to liturgy, with its "radical parallelistic reorientation of all the verbal material as it relates to the building of a sequence" (Waugh 1980, 64). Liturgy emphasizes the poetic function of language, since liturgy includes internal structures of all types (patterning of words and phrases, etc.).[12] Decades ago Stephen Katz emphasized the crucial role of language in not just describing but creating the ritual context for religious experiences, but he lacked the semiotic terminology to explain the power of signs to create a context via the poetic function (1978).

The poetic function of language operates in a hierarchical system with other functions. The Longfellow poem "Hiawatha" if read as part of a filibuster in the United States Senate is not functioning primarily as poetry.[13] So too, liturgies fulfill referential and emotive functions in addition to the poetic. The study of liturgy usually focuses on the referential function, what the prayers are talking about. In the ascent texts, the liturgies not only talk about the heavenly cult but they are also structured as a model of the heavens.

---

11 In Roman Jacobson's definition, "The poetic function projects the principle of equivalence from the axis of selection to the axis of combination" (1960, 358).

12 As one example of emphasizing the poetic function, Segert demonstrates the transformation of prose into poetry, as Ezekiel 1:26 is recast into poetry in 4Q405 20 ii-21–22 with an increased emphasis on meter and structure (1988, 222).

13 A filibuster is a parliamentary procedure by which a single individual extends debate in order to delay or prevent a vote.

In ascent rituals, the liturgy presents, in Peircean terms, a formal icon of the heavenly world. This mapping is an example of ritual hyperstructure which helps account for the power of ritual. "Hyperstructure is the key to this, since ritual actions are not just conventional, they are so conventionalized that they highlight or call attention to the rules, that is to the pattern, model, or semiotic type which the ritual action instantiates" (Parmentier 1994, 133). The hyperstructure of the liturgy, played out in time as it is recited, places the one speaking the liturgy in the heavens; the heavens are present to the extent that they are represented by the signs—and in this case the words—employed in the rite. "Here" is where the ritual takes place and looking for the "here" somewhere "out there" is a category mistake.

The poetic function builds up "discourse-internal iconicities" (G. Urban 1991, 101). These structures of comparison, as played out during the time that the ritual takes, reveal that "poetic structure in discourse can guide pragmatic interpretation by helping interactants map propositional stances into interactional ones" (Fleming and Lempert 2014, 489).[14] Parallelism serves a reflexive, metapragmatic function, bringing about the transformational goal of the rite (moving the human through the heavens).[15] Successful ascent is dependent in part on the larger poetic structures of the ritual. Poetics does more than unitize and make comparable chunks of discourse: it helps fashion discourse into a metapragmatic icon, an image of an act imbued with cultural value (Fleming and Lempert 2014, 490).[16] Once again, context-linked efficacy is much more diffuse in these linguistic functions than in, for example, first-person performatives. These diagrams map the progress-through-time of a ritual and invoke the cosmology that is presupposed.

Our two examples of ascent rituals use varying modes of creating the heavenly context for their rites. Both employ the poetic and other, more lexicalized functions of language. The specific ways these are employed differs, as a close analysis will reveal.

---

14 "Basic to the process of entextualization is the reflexive capacity of discourse. ... The metalingual (or metadiscursive) function objectifies discourse by making discourse its own topic; the poetic function manipulates the formal features of the discourse to call attention to the formal structures by which the discourse is organized" (Bauman and Briggs 1990, 73).

15 See Silverstein (1993, 2004).

16 See Silverstein (2004).

Human and Angelic Choruses Sing Together

Liturgy that describes the heavenly world conveys important information about that world. The *Songs* employ specialized and hard-to-translate vocabulary for the angelic forces, as well as the seven heavenly temples with their seven priesthoods and seven chief priests and the innermost part of the temple. Having this intimate knowledge of the heavenly world no doubt increased the stature of the human priests. As stated by Alexander, "[t]he role of the celestial angel-priests validates the role of the terrestrial human priests, who are engaged in a comprehensive *imitatio angelorum*" (Alexander 2006, 16). The central question is the nature of this imitation of the angelic world when it becomes a ritual practice. Based on the preliminary publication of some of the *Songs* fragments by John Strugnell, Morton Smith argued that they were remnants of an ascent text (1981).[17] Carol Newsom similarly posited that the central vision of the celestial high priest in the seventh hymn is not simply a description of the heavens. Instead, the *Songs* present a step-by-step ascent by the individual reciting the text, culminating in a vision of the highest level of the heavenly temple and its cult (Newsom 1985, 59 – 72).[18] Reiterating a theme constant since the discovery of the text, Philip Alexander also posits that the blessing recited by humans in *Song* 6 "implies some sort of mystical 'ascent' to the heavenly temple" (2006, 28).

The question is how to sort descriptions of praise from uses of praise. Bilha Nitzan, for example, distinguishes between two types of praise. In the first, "the praises invoked from all the cosmos express in harmony the magnificence and majesty of God, the creator of the whole universe" (Nitzan 1994, 166). These descriptions repeat biblical models of praise directed at the deity for the sake of praise, or wrapped up with prayer requests. This type of praise makes no claims about an angelic cult or about human participation in that angelic world. The second type, which she characterizes as a "mystical" type that includes the *Songs*, leads humans to an "experience of mystic communion" (Nitzan 1994, 166). Something about the text seems not simply to describe the cult but to point to human participation in the cult. The lines of demarcation between de-

---

17 Smith also offered the first comparison of the *Songs* with the later *hekhalot* hymns, (1981, 412), a comparison that is taken up in the final section of this paper.

18 Newsom (1990) changed her mind on the question of whether the text was produced specifically for the group living at Qumran, since the appearance of a version of the text at Masada belies a narrow sectarian origin.

scription and participation remain murky and open to debate.[19] Nitzan has located a point of contrast, but the specific classifications remain in debate.

Esther Chazon accepts Nitzan's model but offers some modifications. Chazon distinguishes among (1) the general, biblical model of praise choruses familiar from Nitzan's first category, (2) two distinct choruses (angelic and human), and (3) one chorus that specifically joins humans and angels (2003). Chazon's Type 1 repeats Nitzan's first category, a familiar Biblical trope with Psalm 148 as the paradigm for this type of liturgy (2003, 37). Distinguishing Chazon's second and third types in the *Songs* is much more difficult: the identities and number of the members of the choruses are often obscure. Chazon's first example of Type 2 (two choruses) reads: "[We] the sons of your covenant shall praise ... with all troops of [light]" (*Daily Prayers* [4Q503]). The number of distinct choruses here is indeterminate even though this is her main point of demarcation from Type 3. The vague terms used to identity groups do not help. The term "troops of the light," Chazon argues, "evidently serves here as an epithet for the angels associated with the heavenly lights" (2003, 39).[20] More type 2 from *Blessings* (4QBerakot) differentiate between human praise (4QBerb 3 2 and 4QBerb 5 11) and angelic praise (4QBera 2 4 and 4QBera 7 i 7). Only some angels recite God's holy and glorious name (Chazon 2003, 40–41). All of these examples can be read not as distinct choruses but as pointing to internal hierarchy and stratification. Not all angels or humans take on the same liturgical roles at the same time. Her final example is from *Songs of the Sabbath Sacrifice*. Even when "joint praise is mentioned explicitly in one passage" (4Q400 2 1–7), this example still does not meet her criteria for a single chorus (Chazon 2003, 41).

The third classification, one human/angelic chorus, appears in *Thanksgiving Hymns* (*Hodayot*).[21] These hymns meet her criteria when, and only when, they include first-person "I" or "me" statements, the term "together," or both of these (Chazon 2003, 43). The speaker in the *Self-Glorification Hymn*, for example, asks, "Who is like me among the heavenly beings?" (Chazon 2003, 44). This classification relies on words with obvious contextual implications, such as "you" and "I."[22] Chazon is drawing our attention specifically to context-related explicit

19 Eliot Wolfson rejects her classification of the texts as mystical because of his extremely narrow definition of mysticism, pointing to the circularity found in many discussions of mysticism (1994).

20 She notes other phrases that suggest conjoint worship: "host of angels" (frg. 65), "those who testify with us" (frgs. 11, 15, 65), and "those praising with us" (frgs. 38, 64).

21 On communal human/angelic prayer, see also Chazon (2000).

22 Words dependent on their context for their meaning are often called "deictics" as well as "indexical." See Lee (1997, 358).

indexicals but these are only one small sub-set of the context-linkages. In other words, she has drawn her category too narrowly, relying too much on reference and not enough on other means by which a human/angelic chorus is created.

As noted above, it is the indexical interpretations that are most likely to be lost as the historical context changes.[23] The diagrammatic icon presented in a ritual text may be interpreted as an architectural order, that is, in Peircean terms a rhematic iconic legisign. For those who use the text, however, the map of the heavenly world is a dicent indexical legisign that locates the speaker into the heavenly world (Ball 2014, 160). The concept of dicentization is particularly helpful in articulating how humans become embedded in distinct other-worldly cosmologies, and the controversies around these types of interpretive moves. Specifically, "signs in ritual and other modes of action are semiotically transformed by social actors from icons, or relations of similarity, into indexes, or signs of actual contiguity, through dicentization" (Ball 2014, 168). Tracking the processes of dicentization outlines the capacity of rituals to bring about actual contiguity with, in our examples, the angelic cult.

In the *Songs*, dicentization is reinforced at many levels in many distinct but intersecting ways. Even in fragmentary form, the *Songs* evince an elaborate iconic map of the heavenly cult that coordinates with ritual practices. According to Newsom, the hymns may have been intended for recitation on the first thirteen Sabbaths of the year, organized as two sets of six hymns with a central, most important seventh (Newsom 1985, 1).[24] Alternately Ra'anan Boustan describes the seventh song as the "narrative hinge;" the first six *Songs* focus on the angels while the second half shifts to descriptions of the temple structures engaged in praise (Boustan 2004, 201).[25] Praise permeates the heavens, tying not only the architecture to the angels but also tying all of these actors and actions to the basic linguistic model of the text: praise. This structure of the entire text is a self-reflexive verb writ large, a diagrammatic figuration of praise, with that praise articulated over the time-sequence of the text as at the start, as in any effective ritual. Movement through the text is movement through the heavens.

---

23 See page 7.

24 Although the Priestly source generally portrays this sacrificial system as silent, see references to songs sung on the Sabbath in 2 Chronicles 29:27–28, Sabbath songs attributed to David in 11QPsa 27:5–9, and a Sabbath song mentioned in *Words of the Luminaries*, 4Q504 1–2.

25 Boustan emphasizes that basic affinity made in these songs between the angels and the Temple and refers to this "angelification." Angels have many other roles which are not included in this text, so it is not a broad notion of becoming like the angels but one that focuses on liturgical roles.

Table 1

Songs 1–6	Song 7	Songs 8–13
Liturgists: Speaker plus angels	Pivot to wider circle of liturgists	Everyone and everything participates in heavenly liturgy
Movement: upwards combination of humans and angels		Linear and circular progression into the innermost heavenly circles

At another level, self-reflexive praise verbs begin each composition, activating the diagrammatic figurations. Explicit first- and second-person indexicals, like *You Are Here* signs, appear only in the first two songs. These signs locate the person at the start of a tour circuit. Newsom posits that these terms drop out as the human liturgist becomes increasingly merged with the angelic (Newsom 1985, 14). That is, once the liturgy is launched, the poetic iconic liturgical structure links the reciter to shifting levels of cult; the tour of the heavenly world enacted via the recitation of the liturgy leads the participant into increasingly holy territory.

At yet another level of efficacy, the text maps a confusing hierarchy of social groupings that rework any simple human/divine divide. Instead liturgy's reciters are recalibrated into an array of types of beings. Some sense of hierarchy emerges from special description or inner placement, but many terms remain vague. Among the trickiest are plurals of divine beings, such as *elim* (plural of *el*, "god") and *Elohim*. *Elohim* is used for both the deity and what may be translated "angels." Given this situation, Newsom has chosen to translate the construct form *elohey* into a variety of phrases, including "godlike ones,"[26] "heavenly beings,"[27] and "angels."[28] The vague terms are ambiguous about membership. Newsom notes, "There is a certain ambiguity in the term *kedoshim* (holy ones), which might refer either to the few members of the Qumran community or to the angels" (Newsom 1985, 63). The term seems to group beings based on a different set of criteria than these two choices. The *elim*, for example, appear to be cosmic beings who engage in cultic activities. Newsom leaves this term untranslated, the same strategy used by Yadin (1962, 230) in translating the War Scroll: "He established for Himself priests of the inner sanctum, the holiest of the holy ones, [g]od[like] elim, priests of the lofty heavens" (4Q400 1, lines 19–20). Whoever belongs to this group has a particularly high status.

---

26 "O you godlike ones among all the holiest of the holy ones" (4Q400 1, line 2).
27 "to the King of heavenly beings" (4Q402.3, line 12).
28 "Camps of angels" (4Q401.14, line 8).

Song 2 states: "*Elim* are honored among all the camps of godlike beings and reverenced by mortal councils, a w[onder] beyond godlike beings and mortals (alike)" (4Q400 2, lines 2–3).[29]

The enumeration of diverse categories of heavenly figures occurs in other texts from the Qumran collection. Eileen Schuller, discussing the terminology of the Thanksgiving Psalms/*Hodayot*, notes that the "beloved ones" whose job it is to praise the deity include both humans and angels (1999, 77).[30] Similarly, 1QSbs (*Blessings*, = 1Q28b) offers a priestly blessing that merges humans and angels, elevating humans into the ranks of the highest beings:

> May the Lord bless you and set you as a splendid ornament in the midst of the Holy ones. ... May you be as an angel of the Presence in the holy Abode for the glory of God of hos[ts]. May you attend upon the service in the Temple of the kingdom and decree destiny with the angels of the Presence, and may you be in common council [with the holy ones] for eternal time and for all everlasting ages. (iii. 25–26, iv. 24–26)

A variant reading of the War Scroll (4QMa) describes an individual who becomes one of the *elim* via an ascent (M. Smith 1990). The phrase "I shall be reckoned with gods and established in the holy congregation" is a brag that, as Morton Smith points out, makes most sense coming from someone originally mortal than from an angel (1990).[31] This transformation stretches any standard human/divine dichotomy. Throughout the Qumran texts, some terms pertain to social roles, such as "ministers of the presence," "inhabitants of the highest heights," "chief priests," and "princes." At times the terms indicate activities usually associated with humans, including "*nasi*/prince," "*am bina*/people of discernment," and "*maskil*/teacher" (Fletcher-Louis 2002, 256–257, 282, 298). Other terms are quite vague, such as "pure ones," "holy ones," and "eternal holy ones."[32]

The terms reflect a spectrum of types of divine beings and not a simple human/divine dichotomy. A similar spectrum undergirds Late Antique notions of gender, which was an achieved status that had to be repeatedly performed

---

29 The extensive Late Antique evidence shows that Mizrachi's assumption that humans are by nature excluded from the inner sanctum is too simple (Mizrachi 2015).

30 These compositions fit into Chazon's Type 3, the combined human and angelic choir. The hymns toggle between elaborate deference (who am I?) and audacious status claims.

31 Fletcher-Louis argues that the humans do not ascend but instead engage in heavenly worship on earth, which negates the basic cosmology of multiple heavens and the location of the most important praise as that carried out in heaven in the heavenly temple (2002). For a range of additional critiques of this argument, see Alexander (2006, 45–47).

32 On the terms, see Alexander (2006, 17, 22).

to be confirmed.[33] Male and female were not so much a strict dichotomy as points on a fluid spectrum. Action determined placement on the spectrum: men who act like women will move toward the female end of the spectrum and vice versa. Men could potentially degrade themselves into women, and so too women could achieve male status, even if this did not occur on a regular basis. So too the human–divine continuum marked out many stages of human into divine status (and the reverse) as outlined in Table 2.

Table 2

Intelligible world		Divine world
fleshly bodies	less fleshly bodies	no bodies
human sphere	more divine/less human sphere	divine sphere
humans most men, all women	gods special men heavenly bodies angels (male) divine powers	Deity
human by nature	immortal by gift from Deity	divine by nature

Ascent rituals move participants along this spectrum, whether based on a transformation into a new type of being or a revelation of the true nature of the being. Transformation into a new being by death and resurrection is familiar in later Jewish and Christian theological traditions and therefore not controversial. The possibility that transformation may happen during a lifetime is more controversial; modern notions of ancient Jewish theology only begrudgingly accept the rich range of human/divine categorization found in Late Antique texts. In the first centuries CE the notion of deification "was often expressed with a boldness which surprises moderns who have been brought up to think of the category of divinity as infinitely remote" (Nock 1951, 214). Deification rituals go against modern stereotypes of Judaism and Christianity, and of monotheism. The very idea of human transformation is thought to smack of polytheism and heresy. Nonetheless, transformations along this human–divine spectrum are presented in numerous ancient texts beginning in the first century BCE, effected via burial after death and even while still alive.[34] Rituals could move humans toward the

---

33 See Satlow (1996) and Moore and Anderson (1998) for discussion of Late Antique examples; see Laqueur (1990) for a general outline of the model.
34 See M. Smith (1983, 1990).

divine end of the spectrum, including, to cite only a few examples for their diversity, ascent (Philo, *QE 29*.40), the Taurobolum (Prudentius, *Peristeph.* 10.1048), use of a special belt (Testament of Job 38:3), drowning in the Nile (Vout 2005), and the funeral rites for a Roman emperor as described by Herodian (Gradel 2002).

The *Songs* draw on Ezekiel's "definition of the cultic duty of the priests: to approach God in order to serve him" (Mizrachi 2015, 53). The notion of "drawing near" has been totally reimagined. This rethinking is overdetermined, that is, it comes from several motivations including shifting cosmological presuppositions and the greater possibility of human to divine transformation.

Table 3: Classification from Songs

human		to		divine
Humans	Priests	Some angels; some human priests heavenly chorus	Elim; special priests who draw nearest to the deity (Mizrachi 2015)	Angel of the Presence

The new interpretations of the priestly role are described and discussed in numerous texts but are made into liturgy in the *Songs*. That is, our central question is: Why make the content of liturgy the liturgical actions of heavenly beings? The heavenly cult has been re-imagined. Cult is now a "speech act" verb of praising writ large, with every part of the heavenly world, the angels as well as the other heavenly entities from thrones and on, are all engaged in liturgical practices. This dramatic re-presentation of heavenly action enacts a reinterpreted heavenly cult which in turn undergirds a new earthly set of actions. The temple is a site of praise and is unified by means of praise. To return to the issue of seemingly missing techniques for ascent, ritual technique may appear to be lacking because the *Songs* present a words-only priestly version of ascent.

The presentation of the heavenly sacrificial cult is a priestly totalizing reinterpretation of the cult in scriptural texts. The heavenly buildings have been remade in the image of the praising priests. This point may seem obvious because the heavenly chorus becomes so familiar in later rabbinic texts, but it is a striking reinterpretation of the sacrificial cult. In the *Songs*, all the non-priestly elements of sacrifice, such as the individual who brings the sacrifice, have been eliminated from the picture.

The *Songs* do not include any specific citations of angelic liturgy. Alexander surveys and rejects many of the explanations for this lack of direct citation of angelic liturgy, arguing that silence may be attributed to the highest level of angels (Alexander 2006, 113–115).[35] References to silence are rare in the text however.[36] Instead of citing specific lines of liturgy, the *Songs* present a rich vocabulary of verbal actions. These actions are mapped onto the various parts of the heavenly world by reference to types of praise activity and not by direct citation. The heavenly world is said to extol, announce, exult, the deity by means of words, songs, psalm, and praise. All of these types of action are incorporated into the *Songs* self-reflexively as the *Songs* are all of those types of actions. The work of the text is not to tell us what the angels say but to turn everything into the self-reflexive action of praising.

A spoken words-only ritual text may seem to be the most democratic version of an ascent ritual possible, since it lacks any frame that limits the ritual to a certain clientele. The text might appear to be efficacious for every reader. The liturgy, however, may assume a priestly liturgist and even a very restricted type of priestly reciter. Mizrachi argues that the unusual term "Priests of the >QWRB," translated "priests of the inner sanctum" by Newsom, may refer to priests with special status. These priests were marked by their capacity to "draw near" the deity (Mizrachi 2015).[37] The rite might be understood to work only for those who are capable of "drawing near" without dire consequences. This group has not only priestly status but special qualifications necessary for their participation in the highest levels of cult and the rite may have been their purview. Mizrachi's analysis supports the idea that the liturgy was not part of standard cultic practice—for example, in early synagogues—but instead reflects one priestly vision among what may have been many.

For some priests, joining in the heavenly cult would have been an obvious continuation of the prior priestly tradition; where cult is, there go priests. Being a priest meant being ready to serve not only on earth but in the highest level of the cosmic temple as well. Some priests no doubt had their own basis for claims of special status over and against other priests and other religious practitioners.

---

35 See also Mizrachi (2015, 47). The extensive direct citation of angelic liturgies in the *hekhalot* texts is discussed in the next section.
36 See one of only a few references: "They announce in the quiet" *Songs* frag 1, col II.
37 For instances of the term in the *Songs*, see Mizrachi (2015, 38).

Divine Words of Praise: Humans Sing Angelic Liturgy

A different model of ascent appears in the loosely defined corpus of *hekhalot* (palace) texts.[38] These texts were transmitted distinct from the more well-known rabbinic texts. Moulie Vidas associates the collections with the figure of the *tanna'im*/reciter, well known from the Babylonian Talmud (Vidas 2013).[39] The majoritarian stance of the Babylonian Talmud belittles these ancient text specialists as mere reciters. These individuals are demeaned as mindless repeaters who know a great deal of material by heart but are unable to expound the inner meanings of the Torah (Vidas 2013, 141–142). Their textual limitations are matched by a vividly imagined destructive capacity; reciters are described as "destroyers of the world" (Sotah 22a), among other negative phrases (Vidas 2013, 144). These negative portrayals were, presumably, not shared by the figures themselves. They championed their own liturgical and ritual practices, and had their own views about the investigation of the Torah with their distinct "Torah ethos" (Vidas 2013, 77).

Reconstructing minority views is extremely difficult in a majoritarian text. It is difficult to even understand the battle lines; rabbis often attack their opponents by exaggerating their differences or making their targets obscure (Janowitz 1997). They distort the concerns and approaches to the Torah of the *hekhalot* circles. Reciting by heart is devalued or perhaps those who are known for reciting by heart are devalued, despite both the foundational role of text recitation and the reciters' engagement in other activities such as interpretation.[40] Vidas labels the minority *hekhalot* version of Torah study as "magic," a label that continues the rhetorical denigration of the voices in the Babylonian Talmud (Vidas 2013, 77). Once again, semiotic analysis offers greater precision for comparison, both with the earlier ascent texts and with differing conceptions of normative textual pragmatics (use of words, embodiment of Torah).

Similar to the *Songs*, the angelic cult is the ritual engine in the later ascent rituals. Unlike in the *Songs*, however, in these text the recitation of specific angelic liturgical formulas is central. Specific and lengthy citations from angelic liturgy supply the fuel for ascent. In *Ma'aseh Merkavah* (The Working of the Chariot), for example, a dialogue between a "student" rabbi and a "teacher" rabbi

---

38 See page 88 above.

39 The term *tanna* comes from the verb to repeat or learn. Translations of the term "tanna" vary widely and include Sage or Reciter.

40 Vidas cites the work of Neil Danzig, who argues that the term *tannaim* was also used for scholars who engaged in a variety of text-related activities, not just rote memorization (2013, 144).

both teaches and effects the ascent. The prayer formulas (such as "You will be blessed") are framed not only as reported speech but as reported dialogues or, more correctly, the reports of reported dialogues. The text weaves together the dialogic frames and the direct citation of specific angelic praise formulas that include the divine name, once again embedded in the heavenly hierarchy.[41]

The text's diagrammatic figuration is elaborate:

Rabbi Ishmael said,   [outermost narrative frame]
    I asked Rabbi Akiba a prayer that a man does when ascending. He said to me:
                                [report of a dialogue]
            Purity and holiness are in his heart. ... He prays a prayer
                                [report of the content of that dialogue]
        You will be blessed, [etc.] [reported formula]

The frame explicitly connects the recitation of the prayers and the ascent, self-reflexively outlining the requirements for ascent that the prayers will then instantiate. In this version of ascent, Rabbi Akiba states that the requirements for ascent are a pure heart and the proper formula. While later writers, such as the tenth-century Hai Gaon, associated fasting techniques with ascent, in this rite the recitation of angelic liturgy is the main engine for the ascent.[42] The pure heart requirement adds a neat, impossible-to-test requirement alongside the formulas, as in the previous ascent ritual the ascender may have an elevated status of some type. Via the recitation of the prayers, Akiba joins the heavenly chorus. Morton Smith, analyzing a different *hekhalot* text, astutely observed that when Rabbi Nehunya's companions want to ask him a question they must carefully interrupt him, because he is not simply talking about an ascent but ascending while he talks (1963, 145).[43]

The dialogic frames are cast as reported speech, sometimes referred to as represented speech.[44] Represented speech is an extraordinarily complex strategy, rich in association in this cultural setting. Much of rabbinic literature is also represented speech, where debate and retort statements are attributed to speakers both named and anonymous. The authors are troping off the represent-

---

41 In this version of "performativity" there is no distinction between use and mention of divine names. See the prohibition against speaking the divine name even as a witness in court Sanhedrin 7:5 and b. Sanhedrin 91a. Compare b. Sanhedrin 55a. See Janowitz (1993).

42 In the extant Hekhalot literature "... fasting is not explicitly prescribed for the purpose of the vision of the Merkavah" (Swartz 1994, 145).

43 For the text, see Schäfer, Schlüter, and Mutius (1981); and for a translation without the framing devices marked, see Davila (2013, 37–157).

44 On reported speech, see Lee (1997, 166–67).

ed speech of the Torah, where large parts of the text are presented as the reported speech of the deity spoken by Moses. In all these cases reported speech is "Self-consciously emblematic of its authenticity" even while "transferring the aura of historical objectivity and representational naturalness from inner to outer frame of discourse" (Parmentier 1993, 263).[45]

These linguistic forms constitute one layer of the text's multi-layered efficacy. The device of reported speech, when combined with rabbinic ideas about effective words, results in a didactic text that conveys not only knowledge about but success in ascent. That is, the prayers include recitation of divine names, a central liturgical fuel for rabbinic prayers. According to the rabbis, the deity spoke his name when he created the world.[46] In short, the divine name is the maximally-creative linguistic form, so is subject to stringent taboos. The term *Shem Ha-Meforash* is a shorthand reference for the process of divine naming, both as the Name refers to the deity and as it is an instrument of creativity. Exegesis of the Name is exegesis of all of the deity's power bundled in a single word. The choice of name is obvious since the name is the word which most closely "stands for" the deity, the most powerful and the most subject to taboos. The nature of divine-name power and the subsequent taboos is such that "The more intense the interdiction, the more power seems to accrue to the transgressive act" (Fleming and Lempert 2011, 5).

By uttering all sorts of name-substitutes, even at the level of sounds, the power of the names can be conferred on humans. God's name can be employed in all the variant forms presented in the text, none of which are the name which cannot be used (the Name which warrants a name). The power of the name, with the accompanying taboos, heightens its efficacy. The names seem to have their efficacy "coiled tight inside" (Fleming and Lempert 2011, 6).[47]

If the divine name constitutes one end of the performative spectrum, the diagrammatic figurations of reported speech constitute the other. In this case the figuration includes reports of the organization of the heavens, descriptions of the angels, and direct citations of the liturgy. "As interdiscursive operators, reported speech constructions may seek to diagrammatically reconfigure their surround, recreating the world in their image" (Lempert 2007, 260). The mix of frames and specific formulas builds a structure of both the heavens and movement through the heavens. This "[u]tterance and discourse-level dialogicality can stand for and

---

45 See the discussion in Lempert (2007, 264).
46 This is a post-biblical interpretation. The Scriptural texts prohibit the improper use of the deity's name but contain no prohibition against speaking it.
47 The avoidance registers that emerge around verbal taboos also naturalize convention (Parmentier 1994, 10).

help precipitate large-scale social relations" (Lempert 2007, 269). In this case the social relations include student/teacher instruction and liturgy spoken by humans and angels.

The extremely limited contextual needs outlined in the text reinforce the effectiveness of the prayers, when the heart is pure. Efficacy is established for the original recitation of each formula by report (It worked!). If the formulas were indeed successful on some previous occasion, and the only other necessity is the pure heart of the reciter, then word will equal deed in all the subsequent recitations. The frames do not point to or index any external connections beyond those established by the reported-speech situations. The rituals setting is thus maximally self-contained, dependent on the formulas but little else. In general ritual texts are constructed so as to be free-standing from many possible (local, secular) contextual linkages so as to be recognizable as tokens of distinct types of action with the resulting specific (sacred) contextual linkages. So too, the ascent liturgy strives to set up the most decontextualized, self-contained setting possible since the focus is entirely on the cosmology that is invoked. Teaching thereby becomes use.

Not surprisingly, some versions of ascent rituals direct the efficacy of the words-only rite toward diverse goals, adding new techniques and results. Rabbi Nehunya's ascent, described in Hekhalot Rabbati, has been reedited into a new frame promising that the ascent hymns will enable the reciter to, for example, know what the future holds. The ascent ritual was been edited to include references to fasting, and the flow is interrupted by narrative interludes (Hekahlot Rabbati 424). Sar Ha-Torah/Prince of the Torah rites, aimed at effortless assimilation of Torah and rabbinic teachings are appended to ascents (Swartz 1994, 142).

The ability to work the cosmology, to go up and down at will, becomes a tool that permits the ascender to achieve a myriad of decidedly this-worldly goals. The multifunctionality of the rite is acknowledged in Hekhalot Rabbati when Nehunya says that knowing the ritual is like having a ladder in one's home. Ascent has become routinized. The world of the angels remains the apex of the cosmology, and anyone traversing it is likely to confront the numerous dangers inherent in getting closer to divine power. But the path is potentially open to anyone who has the text. If the Songs were a priestly tool, the question of credentials for ascending has been completely reinterpreted.

Although the normative stance of the rabbis in the Babylonian Talmud condemns the hekhalot circles, the former share the vast majority of the latter's theological precepts. What the two do disagree about is how to use texts, how words function, and the relationship between words and actions. They are engaged in what we may call a "folk debate" about performativity (Fleming and

Lempert 2014, 498). Some rabbis see the tannaim as engaging in magic, which in this case means misunderstanding primarily how words function. Like Plotinus, they do not approve of certain uses of formulas and divine names in rituals (both ascent and Sar-HaTorah), viewing adjurations as taboo uses of language. The seemingly instantaneous transformation of a tanna into a repository of extensive texts is viewed with suspicion. This suspicion is warranted from the rabbis' point of view since divine names are surrounded by taboos and their use by an opponent would be either heresy or magic. This is a point of view the hekhalot circles would reject.

A vision of the heavenly world and recall of copious textual material might have been the goals for everyone, but how those were to be achieved was disputed. All rabbis saw themselves as walking Torahs, with numerous anecdotes paralleling the study of a rabbi's life with studying a holy text. The Talmudic rabbis were committed to the role of the Talmud itself, entextualizing the ritual goals within the larger stretches of Talmudic debate. This investment in the text may appear to be more rational and less magical, but it simply represents another end of the spectrum of performativity: "The poetic and the taboo represent two poles of performative form and function, ranging from the most textually distributed and diffuse, the poetic, to the most localizable and essentialized, the taboo" (Fleming and Lempert 2014, 486). The hekhalot circles essentialize the texts as if it were a name that could be easily memorized and its power thereby made available for use.

The rabbis who ultimately frame the debate were trying to build their monopoly on Torah power even as they denigrate that of others. This hostile debate may parade as a simple historical description of practices and views, but that is because the contextual possibilities of represented speech are harnessed to obfuscate the core grounds of debate. The Torah and all derivation rituals can never be shorn of taboos. The rabbis turn their opponents' semiotic ideology into magic since "Prophylactic measures surrounding the mentioning of unmentionables tend to frame the performative power of these utterance-types as inherent to the sign forms themselves, as if their potency were lodged 'in' the material substance of the sign itself" (Fleming and Lempert 2011, 10).

Comparing Ascents

Most striking, both ascent texts emphasize the angelic cult *as the content of human liturgical texts*. Structure and content mirroring each other; the ascent texts function both iconically and indexically to construct the heavenly world and mark human travels through it. This "dicentization is a way to ritual achievement of alternate realities" (Ball 2014, 161).

Despite these similarities, the different rituals reflect variations in the processes of entextualization, that is, "the process of rendering discourse extractable, of making a stretch of linguistic production into a unit—a *text*—that can be lifted out of its interactional setting" (Bauman and Briggs 1990, 73).[48] The hekhalot liturgies incorporate their contexts of use more explicitly than the *Songs* since they explicitly outline the contextual needs and the results of their use.[49] The dicentization of the *Songs* is easier to miss since the text lacks the explicit equivalent to "I now pronounce you man and wife" that the "Rabbi X said and he saw" adds to the text.

Given the widespread imagery of a heavenly temple, it is surprising that we do not find more texts like the *Songs*; the place for priests is in the heavenly world, just as rabbis study in the heavenly rabbinic academy. A priest could see himself as directly inserted into the angelic cult. Later readers, including modern scholars, could interpret the *Songs* as simply an iconic description of the angelic world, based in part on the assumptions (about monotheism, the function of liturgy, etc.) that they brought to the text.

In the *hekhalot* version of ascent, non-priests can see themselves as part of a special group of humans who have access to the heavenly world. Following another major theme of Late Antique religion, special knowledge is the key. The text is built to be as automatically effective as possible, appending only a claim to a pure heart to the liturgies. The rite begins with a call to praise that puts the liturgy into action and builds methodically from there. Its efficacy is ensured by the introductory advertisement recounting its success. Again, ascent is made as automatic as possible, though who could understand and use the text may have been restricted. Those who knew how to recite the words could map their presence "there", whether or not later readers can even agree on where "there" is. The hekhalot ascents posit no special relationship between human priests and the angelic cultic system. The cultic formulas can easily be adopted and recited by anyone, not just priests. The rites are potentially available for anyone who has the required knowledge of how to use angelic liturgy.

Being aware of the semiotic process of dicentization helps explain how cosmologies, even when explicit indexicals are lacking, "can offer a portal to alternate time-spaces, collapsing ... the separation between actors and events located

---

48 See Silverstein and Urban (1996).

49 Richard Bauman and Charles Briggs explain that, "Entextualization may well incorporate aspects of context, such that the resultant text carries elements of its history of use within it" (Bauman and Briggs, 1990, 73).

elsewhere by bringing them into spatiotemporal contiguity" (Ball 2014, 168). Dicentization works in the first text by transposing the human priestly realm into the divine realm, transforming the human priests and their liturgical recitation into part of the angelic cult. In the later, rabbinic ascent rituals, the chain of rabbinic transmission recounted in the (re)telling of an ascent elevates the reciter into the heavenly world via both iconic (mapping) and indexical (context-related) signs. In this case, the model of ritual efficacy is based on the rabbinic linguistic ideology—that is, that angelic liturgy supplies the fuel for ascent. Such is the power of signs. They are able to invoke a heavenly realm and permit some humans to draw near to divinity as part of the very act of praising the deity because that very action is what the heavenly realm consists of in the first place.

6 The Indeterminate Meaning of Burning Man Rituals and Modern Notions of Spirit

Few rituals exemplify or are better test cases for the modern popular notions of "spiritual" discussed in Chapter Four than rituals at the annual Burning Man Festival. The festival began when twenty friends met on Baker Beach in San Francisco in 1986 to burn an eight-foot wooden effigy of a man built by Larry Harvey and Jerry James.[1] Over a period of thirty-five years, Burning Man has transformed into the annual construction and then dismantling of Black Rock City in the Nevada desert (70,000 inhabitants in 2018). In addition to being the single largest gathering in a national park, when operational Black Rock City constitutes the third-largest city in Nevada. The event now operates on a budget in the tens of millions of dollars.[2]

Once again we see the strategic use of ideas of spirit by both participants and researchers. People who go to Burning Man employ the term because they reject familiar forms of organized religion. The term "spiritual" is a readily available hierarchical claim that serves to set the practices of festival participants apart from other, presumably non-spiritual, practices. Participants claim Burning Man is shorn of any ties to stultifying formal regulation and freed of all ideology, combined with notions of a heightened ethical stance. The event is consciously scripted as opposing traditional forms of religious expression. This division greatly oversimplifies both the character of contemporary religious expression outside of Burning Man and the regimentation of activities at Burning Man. Much more interesting than these common claims is the overt ideology of meaninglessness frequently articulated at the festival. This claim is a fascinating example of semiotic ideology, that, as this chapter will argue, is supplemented with a less obvious ideology whereby meaning is contextually-linked, a veritable indexical emphasis.

---

[1] For a short history and summary of Burning Man, see Gilmore (2010, 17–44). See also Shister (2019).

[2] Details on the budget are hard to obtain.

https://doi.org/10.1515/9783110768602-007

Meaning At Burning Man

Every scholarly piece devoted to Burning Man includes a general attack on any simple or unitary meaning for everything that happens during the event.[3] Matt Wray describes Burning Man's "polysemy" as follows:[4]

> [S]heer hybrid strangeness and polyglot weirdness of the participants and performances contradict and challenge one another, and, for a weekend, the desert becomes a contest of meanings. No one interpretation of the event can ever carry the day. If there is a definitive meaning of the Man, it is that there is no definitive meaning.

Four explanations for this polysemy deserve review due to their general popularity: van Gennep's liminality, Victor Turner's antistructure, Mikhail Bakhtin's carnivalesque, and Michel Foucault's heterotopia. All of these capture some general characteristics of Burning Man, but none explain its particular models of interpretation. First, the desert location of Burning Man may seem to represent the essence of liminality in van Gennep's classic definition of rites of passage.[5] Withdrawing from daily life, experiencing the freedom of the desert, and then returning to normal life outlines the basic structure of a rite of passage. The entire event is a drawn-out liminal experience with the creative possibilities that liminality offers. However, van Gennep's capacious model of liminal space suits almost any ritual.[6] As if aware of this problem, Graham St. John describes Burning Man as a "hyper-liminal" performance zone, a slightly altered version of van Gennep's model (St. John 2001, 52). So too, V. W. Turner's reworking (1979) of van Gennep's model as *communitas* is widely cited by participant observers.[7] For example, Lee Gilmore (2010, 100) states, "liminality as subversive, anti-authoritarian, and anti-structural, and his [Turner's] repeated analogies to popular culture render his ideas especially seductive." Turner's twist on van Gennep emphasizes the subversive aspects of the event, but we are in need of something

---

3 Most studies of Burning Man are done by participant observers, many trained in cultural theory. For dissertations on Burning Man see Stevens (2003), Hockett (2004), Green (2009), Clupper (2007), and Noveroske-Tritten (2015). For books, see most recently Shister (2019). I attended Burning Man twice as a participant observer.
4 Cited from St. John (2001, 54). The online version cited there is no longer available.
5 For other general references, see Pike (2005, 206).
6 Frederick Turner's frontier thesis reinforces a specifically American model of a liminal West where comforts are traded for freedom, whether based on an historical description or on a myth (1920). Bowditch (2010, 6) cites Baudrillard's claim that desert space is where a new narrative begins in America.
7 See, for example, Gilmore (2010, 99–100).

more specific that can explain how the event constructs, acts out, and interprets its subversion.[8] Thus, while it is worthwhile to note the many ways in which Burning Man takes place outside social norms in a desert location, van Gennep's model and van Gennep–derived models of analysis are not sufficient to explain the semiotic fluidity of the event.

Another popular model is Bakhtin's carnivalesque, adapted from medieval carnivals (Bakhtin and Holquist 1981).[9] These periods of permitted license had an outsize influence on European society, according to Bakhtin, because the carnivalesque fosters free thinking. What happens when the carnivalesque becomes the norm? Burning Man has a set of ten principles that are firmly established within the community: Radical Inclusion, Gifting, Decommodification, Radical Self-Reliance, Radical Self-Expression, Communal Effort, Civic Responsibility, Leaving No Trace, Participation, and Immediacy.[10] These norms are reinforced by a group of volunteer Rangers, making the festival not so much a period of relaxation of norms as an experiment in a new set of norms.[11]

The final popular model is Foucault's heterotopia, a distinct type of "counter-site" contrasted with the more familiar notion of utopia. Foucault outlines his model thus:

> There are also, probably in every culture, in every civilization, real places—places that do exist and that are formed in the very founding of society—which are something like counter-sites... . Because these places are absolutely different from all the sites that they reflect and speak about, I shall call them, by way of contrast to utopias, heterotopias. (Foucault and Miskowiec 1986)

According to Hetherington, a heterotopia "sets up unsettling juxtapositions of incommensurate 'objects' which challenge the way we think, especially the way our thinking is ordered" (Hetherington 1997, 42). These sites "always possess

---

8 For a darker view of *communitas*, see Zwissler (2011, 333–36), St. John (2001, 48–50), and the classic description of crowds in Canetti (1962).

9 Bakhtin's notion of heteroglossia is also cited. The issue is how a model of voicing from novels translates into rituals that open up a wide range of interpretations. Heteroglossia "resists the didactical process inherent in ideological formation because action is valued over negation enacted by the burn" (Noveroske-Tritten 2015, 16).

10 The Ten Principles of Burning Man are listed on the website and reiterated constantly during the festival: https://burningman.org/culture/philosophical-center/10-principles/. (accessed June 20, 2021).

11 There is also a local police presence in Black Rock City, but participants are more likely to encounter Rangers moving around the city than police.

multiple meanings for agents."[12] Burning Man "consists of a plurality of contradictory and/or complementary discourses and practices—often expressed through heterotopia" (St. John 2001, 51). Specifically, Burning Man is an example of a temporal heterotopia, which breaks "from traditional time and place, simultaneously representing, contesting and inverting the everyday" (Bowditch 2010, 80). Cacophony has certainly been part of Burning Man since the earliest days, when the San Francisco Cacophony Players participated (Clupper 2007, 36).

These models, though all helpful to some extent, are ahistorical and very general in their approach to (linguistic and semiotic) meaning. Our goal is to understand how different forms of multiple meanings and meaninglessness are created through the collective, collaborative, dialogic regimentation of sign interpretation at Burning Man. For example, Happenings were famously considered to be chaotic, freewheeling events, yet they had to follow specific rules in order to be Happenings.[13] Perhaps not explicitly articulated, guidelines existed about how these "disorganized" events should be structured in order to make certain types of events recognizable as Happenings.

Like Happenings, Burning Man has its structuring guidelines. The Ten Principles, handed out to each participant at the entrance to Burning Man, provide one level of an interpretive system. Events taking place at Burning Man are shaped by these principles both in terms of what happens and of how events are framed. Actions that take place in many settings are understood to articulate these values when they occur in Black Rock City. This is a far cry from the idea that events are meaningless. If anything, the City becomes a focusing lens for interpreting many behaviors, thoughts, and actions, including some quite mundane. They are given new meanings by their association with the Principles. Beyond the Principles, we need to search more deeply in order to understand sign interpretation at Burning Man and other ways in which signs are used that may not be obvious to participants.

---

12 For example, ConFest in Australia, an alternative lifestyle and environmental festival, is described as "an *alternative cultural heterotopia*, a matrix of performance zones occupied by variously complementary and competing neo-tribes and identity clusters" (St. John 2001, 48).

13 For Happenings, see Kirby and Dine (1965); for Happenings in relation to Burning Man, Clupper (2007, 91).

The Indeterminacy of Modern Art: Everything is Art

Black Rock City is notable for its public art, as evidenced by the steady stream of books about art at Burning Man.[14] The event is known for the immense sculptures constructed on the playa, a large open space which functions as an outdoor art gallery. Outreach from the event often takes the form of circulating art projects from the playa displayed around the world.[15]

No sharp distinction is drawn between the art on the playa and daily life in the rest of the city, though the playa affords larger spaces for viewing. Everything and anything in the life of the community not only could potentially be art, but *is* art. Drawing on ideas familiar from discussions of both modern and contemporary art criticism, art becomes a frame that can be placed around any item or act. Shifting from the "white cube" of the art gallery, placement within the circular fence that encompasses Burning Man renames all aspects of life "art." As Richard Stevens explains, the participants "are makers not only on the basis of the art but the stuff of art themselves" (Stevens 2003, 145).

Artistic expression is the organizing frame for daily life. Each campsite has some type of display that both identifies and adorns it. The camp themes distinguish each dwelling site from its neighbors in often very elaborate fashion. Clothing is explicitly described as a mode of artistic expression. Participants dress in widely varying styles and many of them create their own outfits. The Free Boutique offers free clothing and helpers to assist with any alterations wanted.[16] The only cars licensed for use are art cars that crawl slowly through the community.

This vision of daily life as art does not just happen by accident. Burning Man life is steeped in conscious experimentation with ideas about art that were worked out in many distinct modern-art movements.[17] The practice of making and giving small art objects, for example, is reminiscent of Joseph Beuys's multiples (Fortunati 2005, 163).[18] Beuys made and distributed multiple copies of the same small constructs; sometimes he added distinguishing flourishes, and other times not. Similarly, Burners make and gift one another small art objects

---

14 See, for example, Raiser (2016) and Harvey (2017).
15 Books that include photos of playa art include Raiser (2016) and Harvey (2017).
16 Denise Green (2009) discusses clothing in Black Rock City especially as the experience of creative dressing carries over to daily life after the event.
17 See, for example, the work of Fluxus (Harren 2016).
18 For multiples, see the Munich Pinakothek der Moderne's Joseph Beuys multiples website (Pinakothek 2021).

(Fortunati 2005, 164).[19] The constant exchange of these small art gifts is the closest the City comes to having a currency.[20] Just as the exchange of ceremonial mats at a funeral constructs a diagrammatic icon of the kinship system, a system that is enacted by the exchange itself, at Burning Man the exchange of these small gifts creates a form of social relation, often between strangers.[21]

The forms of art found at Burning Man include—and, I argue, extend—all the various forms of Post-Movement modern art. The variety of artistic forms articulate with those listed by Rosalind Krauss in the 1970s: performance art, videos, photorealism, monumental sculpture, and abstract painting (Krauss 1977a, 68).[22] Beyond its sheer variety, artistic expression at Burning Man mimics modern-art movements in rejecting any notion of norming style.[23] Krauss describes the wide range of modes of expression as "an image of personal freedom, of multiple options now open to individual choice or will, whereas before these things were closed off through a restrictive notion of historical style" (Krauss 1977a, 68). The demise of any strict notion of style has a centripetal force on choice of materials, modes of production, and every other aspect of artistic expression and evaluation.

With no notion of style, it is hard to distinguish art from nonart. What Arthur Danto states about art after the mid-1960s is true of Burning Man: "it was no longer clear that we could pick the artworks out from the non-artworks all that easily, since art was being made which resembled non-artworks as closely as may be required" (Danto 1998, 129). Echoing Krauss, Danto argued that after Duchamp submitted his "readymade" urinal to an art show, interpretation replaced aesthetics (1998, 133). Interpretation, not style, is the core cultural act that regiments meaning. For Danto, "interpretive seeing" is demanded of viewers. Danto is aware that some level of interpretive seeing was always necessary, based on the social norms for finding meaning in art. He is trying to characterize a new type of "interpretive seeing" which is freed from once-common social (philosophical) restraints. The process of this type of seeing remains somewhat enig-

---

19 This activity brings about the "active mobilization of every individual's latent creativity" (Fortunati 2005, 167).

20 Money is used only to purchase ice and drinks at the central café. All other services, including the post office, are free.

21 For the exchange of funeral mats see Parmentier (1994).

22 Video is less prevalent because of the need to generate electricity.

23 A semiotic understanding of "style" is discussed below. On a point beyond the scope of this chapter, Krauss adapts Walter Benjamin and Roland Barthes to argue that photography supplies the model for readymades and many other contemporary art objects (Krauss 1977a, 75).

matic; Danto states that art is now defined by an "aboutness" that is "embodied" in some form (Danto 1998, 130).

The interpretation of meaning leads once again to semiotics. When Krauss tries to explain in greater detail how modern art is endowed or not endowed with meaning, she turns to the Peircean concept of indexical sign.[24] She defines an indexical sign: "It is a sign which is inherently 'empty,' its signification a function of only this one instance, guaranteed by the existential presence of just this object. It is the meaningless meaning that is instituted through the terms of the index" (Krauss 1977a, 78). In this semiotic view, indexical signs are meaningless because they only "point to" something. A photograph, for example, indexically points to the implied presence of the photographer, but little else. Beyond this indexical pointing a "supplemental discourse" is needed (Krauss 1977a, 59).

For both Krauss and Danto, an urgent question is who is providing this discourse. "Art is about expression: Once art becomes construed as expression, the work of art must send us ultimately to the state of mind of its maker, if we are to interpret it" (Danto 1986, 104). The necessary supplemental discourse may be provided by the artist who provides a long discourse on the meaning of a piece of art. Other supplemental discourses may be added by critics who postulate what the artist had in mind, perhaps in ways that the artist is not aware of. Viewers are free to add their own interpretations as well.

Krauss has put her finger on something central to the indeterminacy of modern art. Her argument anticipates some of the claims made about meaninglessness and negation made at Burning Man. However, Krauss is interpreting a photograph as an index and only a "pointing-to" index. If no supplemental discourse is available, a piece of art remains a meaningless indexical "trace," like the ringing of a telephone when the relationship between the ringing and the physical phone has been broken. The sound signals that something is happening in a specific place, but does nothing beyond directing attention to a specific place.

A photo, contra to Krauss's claims, in addition to pointing has a formal standing-for mode of representation as well. Abstract art, for example, combines indexical pointing-to with formal representation, even if it is of the artistic process itself (as in the case of Jackson Pollock paintings). As one example from Burning Man, Michael Light, in his Full Moon project, arranged digitally enhanced NASA images of the lunar desert, at a 1:1 scale, in the form of a 175-foot landing strip, imprinting the surface of the moon on the Nevada desert (Dyer 2001). Once placed on the sand the photos were indexical (pointing-to) for-

---

24 On indexicals see note 10 in the Introduction.

mal representations (icons) of the lunar surface in an "elision of the actual and photographed desert" (Dyer 2001).

Duchamp bringing the urinal into the art gallery and the process of making objects into readymades are both examples of decontextualizing and then recontextualizing objects.[25] Their status as representations needs to be rearticulated, since they clearly no longer stand for whatever they once did. In the recontextualization that takes place at Burning Man, daily life is art because it takes place there. Everything is thereby set within the focusing lens of Burning Man and its regimentation of meaning. The issue is to characterize that specific form of regimentation, distinguishing it from, for example, earlier notions of style, without agreeing with the claims that everything is either meaningless or that meaning is obvious.

The Contextual Power of Indeterminate Rituals

Attending Burning Man has a powerful impact on participants, with an astounding 65 percent of people reporting in 2016 that the event changed their lives (Fortunati 2005, 163). This level of change, even if exaggerated, is the envy of religious leaders, theater companies, and psychologists. From this vantage point, Burning Man offers a rich opportunity for analysis of rituals, using the particular framing of events at Burning Man to think about efficacy in very broad terms.

Many standard rituals are viewed with suspicion by Burning Man participants, as they are by scholars of religion. This suspicion is based on a long history of associating "ritual" with meaningless actions done by rote.[26] Those who want to emphasize the transformational capacity of rites either localize ritual power in first-person verbs or use the term performative as a substitute for magic. Does Burning Man's emphasis on artistic expression and the power of the regimentation of meaning by non-regimentation give us insights into rituals?

Two clusters of rituals, burnings and weddings, demonstrate how a rite, like style-free indeterminate art, demand supplemental discourse. Most famous in the first group (burnings), is the Man Burn, the burning of a huge human effigy in a display of fireworks and flame.[27] This event is considered by many to be the

---

25 Krauss posits that the readymade "is about the physical transposition of an object from the continuum of reality into the fixed condition of the art-image by a moment of isolation, or selection" (Krauss 1977a, 78).

26 See the Introduction, page 7.

27 Some of the large art pieces are also burned.

highlight of the festival at Black Rock City.[28] The drama of construction and destruction is performed minus explanation or explication. To the oft-repeated question, *What does the burning of a huge effigy of a man mean?* Larry Harvey, one of the founders of the event, answers, "Nothing."[29] This dogged refusal to fix meaning by any standard means of interpretation is labeled "ritual without dogma" by (Gilmore 2010, 68). But rituals without dogma still have both efficacy and extensive interpretations. Harvey's claim does not begin to illuminate the many meanings of the rite for participants, how the rite represents, for example, the Ten Principles or the changes that it brings about.

For many, the burning of a figure imports a tapestry of meanings from the long history of animal, human, and modified sacrifice traditions. The Man Burn then being a token of a familiar type.[30] The Burn is a moment of solidarity and communion, a gift, a form of purification, a transformation of some aspect of a person, or the destruction of something that needs to be disposed of.[31] The effigy can be a scapegoat in place of those who watch it burn, a body on its way to a new existence, or a moment expressing *Wow!* Like the artist or critic explaining a new art installation, participants are eager to expound on what they think the Man stands for even if their lengthy explanations begin with a nod toward meaninglessness. Simply put, the Man Burn can be understood to *undermine or support* all the interpretations listed and any others that can be imagined.

None of these meanings are inherent in the act but meanings are easily associated with it in the same manner that notions of "sacrifice" motivate and explain many forms of selective destruction in religious rituals. Citing Alfred Loisy, Valerio Valeri describes ritual *"efficacious representation."* No single idea will ever encompass all of the possible ways of interpreting this type of efficacious destruction. Understanding the power and potential meanings of these rites requires "less a theory of the gift than a theory of representation" (Valeri 1985, 67). A semiotic theory of sacrifice begins thus not with a specific idea such as a gift to the gods, but with the question of how the elements "stand for" something else that is thereby incorporated into the rite and transformed.[32] Every act of sacrifice is thus itself already a representation of change of some sort, that is, "the crucial fact is that it is an icon" (Valeri 1985, 67).

---

28 The rite is discussed by Gilmore (2010, 70–83).
29 He has repeated this claim in numerous interviews (Bowditch 2010, 30).
30 For the token/type distinction, see Parmentier (1994, 132–33).
31 For these interpretations and others, see Valeri (1985), Lee and LiPuma (2002), and Carter (2003).
32 Hubert and Mauss (1899) offer a theory of sacrifice that highlights issues of representation.

Taking Valeri's analysis and putting it into Peircean terms, the specifics of representation are only partially regimented, or they are regimented by a fluid sense of both indexicality and iconicity. If style is a form of cross-contextual regimentation, there is no "style" to interpreting transformation at Burning Man (Parmentier 1997, 77). There is no consistency of interpretation (as found in legisigns) beyond the Ten Principles. Every item to be transformed must be brought in and all of the remains must be carried out again, marking the start and the end.

The Burns are indexical icons: indexical because they point to all the presences that co-occur at the event and icons because all these interpretations see the Burn as the formal representation of something. Efficacious representation goes all the way down through the layers of culture. The creation and destruction of Black Rock City is mirrored in all the smaller creations and destructions. As praise was the basic model for liturgies of ascent, transformation understood as creation, then destruction, is the model for everything at Burning Man, with both the stage of creation and the stage of destruction offering creative opportunities for reconfiguration of sign meaning.

In another act of burning, every year a temple is constructed and then burned at the end of the week. The building is easily recognizable as a temple based on its placement in the playa, its size, and the use of elements found in diverse religious structures.[33] The Temple is a site of constant activity during the week. Visitors post photos of deceased relatives and friends, leave small memorabilia inside and around the building, and inscribe names and farewell wishes on the structure with colored pens. They sit in silence, chant or sing, or engage in very individual acts of mourning, such as one person who played a melody on bagpipes while walking around the interior space.[34]

David Best, the architect of many of the most recent temples, built the first Temple to memorialize a participant's death in a motorcycle accident (Bowditch 2010, 227). Best imagined the Temple as a site for memorializing suicides, since religious traditions often exclude them. No theological slogans are permitted. The Temple repeats elements from other temples that participants are likely to have encountered.

Sarah Pike argues that the practices at the Temple recall a past when death was part of daily life and not sanitized. However, the nature, as well as the transience, of the Burning Man camp means that the population of the dying is missing. Some participants discuss the Burning Man Temple as a place for scattering

---

33 For more discussion, see Pike (2005), Bowditch (2010, 223–44), and Gilmore (2010, 87–94).
34 See the descriptions in Shister (2019, 83–87, 142–43).

their ashes, but few described wanting to come there to die. Common Temple activities do not include any end-of-life practices or the presence of the dying or corpses. After a participant ran into the Man Burn and died, volunteers guard the perimeters of the fire to prevent additional suicides. Death is still sanitized even as all forms of emotional expression of mourning are welcomed. The Temple does offer a capacious site for mourning. The Temple was generally at the quiet end of the noise spectrum at Burning Man, with what can be called a somber mood (for the burning as well).[35] Yet mourning took on very individual forms of expression, including the posting of photos and names.[36] Many individuals engaged in other types of mourning rites in other settings, yet they found participation in the Temple to be meaningful as well.

Numerous ideas are associated with the Temple's construction and destruction. Its burning is a sign of impermanence, a site for "working through" mourning in the Freudian sense, and a mechanism for communicating with other worlds and the dead. The Temple can support or critique other practices depending on the particular individual's view. Some see the new version of the type as permanently and completely displacing older visions of temples; others do not.

Burning the Temple is one more icon of the creation/destruction model, indexically linked to the unique location. All the objects placed inside the Temple are burned with the building. Wittingly or not, this act solves the problem of what to do with items that have been employed in a ritual setting. It is easier to sacralize an object than desacralize it. In contrast to the Temple Burn, the National Park Service must decide whether to store or dispose of every item left at the Vietnam Veterans Memorial and other memorials.[37]

Burning Man weddings constitute a second cluster of ritual. Modern weddings, as anyone reading the "Vows" pages of the *New York Times* notes, reflect greater individualization and detraditionalization (Hoesly 2015, 8).[38] Many contemporary weddings are cross-cultural. Leeds-Hurwitz uses a wide variety of terms to capture the eclectic nature of these weddings, including mosaic, salad bowl, coat of many colors, bricolage from Lévi-Strauss (Leeds-Hurwitz 2002, 180), along with syncretism, hybridity, creolization, third-culture building (Leeds-Hurwitz 2002, 255n7). These weddings, "have multiple meanings simulta-

---

35 Thus the tone is very different from the growing trend of End of Life parties to celebrate someone's death as they prepare to die.

36 Best, as noted above, saw the site as a place for mourning any and every death, including those such as suicides.

37 See the National Park Service website (NPS 2021).

38 See also Freedman (2015) and Hoesly (2015, 3).

neously and everyone need not attend to the same meaning" (Leeds-Hurwitz 2002, 219).

Officiants also no longer represent main-stream religious traditions. The Universal Life Church (ULC), founded in 1959 by Kirby J. Hensley, is a fast track credentialing for officiants.[39] It was a very American moment when a religious organization was able to get approval for a nondenominational credential, made easily available for citizens who want to officiate at a wedding. Aaron Sankin characterizes the church thus: "The Universal Life Church is possibly the most quintessentially American religion of the internet age. It's one based on equal parts sincere religious devotion, shameless hucksterism, and a radical belief in near total openness" (Sankin 2015).

The Church has ordained more than twenty million officiants (Hoesly 2015, 9).[40] Of those ordained, 80 to 90 percent do so in order to officiate at the wedding of a friend or relative (Hoesly 2015, 5). A much smaller percentage seeks ordination for fun (Hoesly 2015, 6).[41] Couples turn to friends and relatives because they are interfaith or gay and unable to find traditional officiants (Hoesly 2015, 3) or because they are seeking what they think will be a more personalized and meaningful ceremony (Hoesly 2015, 7).

Weddings at Burning Man reflect all of these trends. The wedding section of the Burning Man website states, "There are no legal requirements concerning what you must do or say at your wedding. Create any sort of ritual, game, or party you like."[42] Universal Life Church officiants conduct many Burning Man weddings. Participants may opt for the ULC because they are pragmatic; someone wishing to be an officiant can register in three minutes on the Universal Life Church website.

The wedding of Ninja and Tijuana is one example of a Burning Man wedding, chosen because the participants were willing to talk about their ceremony.[43] According to their report, this wedding took only a few hours to plan and carry out, though this does not include getting the license and gathering all the items used in the ceremony (e.g., champagne). The wedding's structure included a traditional diagrammatic figuration. Anyone coming upon the ceremo-

---

39 This form of credentialing is easier and less expensive than registering with the state for authority to marry.
40 Forty-eight states permit ULC officiants to officiate at weddings.
41 The two goals are not mutually exclusive. Hoesly (2015, 4) recounts first joining the ULC for fun and then agreeing to officiate at weddings.
42 See the Burning Man website (2021).
43 The wedding party included the author of a dissertation on Burning Man, Linda Noveroske-Tritten. Details were reported during a conversation with Linda Noveroske-Tritten.

ny would quickly grasp that it was a wedding, a small gathering arranged around a couple and an officiant, complete with aisle. The bride walked down the aisle, vows were exchanged, the officiant made a statement and declared the couple wed, followed by the smashing of a glass.[44]

If the form was familiar, the specific details connected the event specifically with Burning Man. Burners filled traditional the family role of giving away the bride.[45] The couple were referred to as Ninja and Tijuana, their playa names, given by other Burners based on an event or encounter.[46] During the ceremony the couple referred to the fact that they met at Burning Man. They exchanged Burning Man tags instead of rings, defining themselves in terms of their Burning Man identities and rejecting the imagery of rings.

The vows were a web of self-reflexive statements, with constant direct "pointing to" the immediate context via references to Black Rock City, the playa, and Burners present and absent. The vows outlined the social group, describing it as a "community of like-minded people" and stating that "we are all Burners." Ninja used an iPhone to display a series of photographs that illustrated the vows he had composed. Many of the photos displayed by Ninja were of other events at Burning Man, creating a very specific history in the way in which cosmology and history are included in the language of traditional religious weddings. The phone was used to archive the couple's relationship and articulate a history and a set of values. Tijuana also addressed the history of Burning Man, describing it as a "heterotopia."

The wedding enacted many Burning Man principles. Based on Radical Inclusion, anyone walking by becomes an automatic invitee to the wedding. Such occurrences happen frequently when a wedding is on the playa or near the Temple. People who pass by may just continue on by or may join the ceremony and participate for as long as they want and then move on. The majority of participants at a reception may not know each other, being people happening to stroll past when the reception began.

The wedding was a legally binding event and thus interacted with the Principle of Civic Responsibility. According to this principle, "[participants] must also assume responsibility for conducting events in accordance with local, state and federal laws." Most Burning Man civic organizations and events oper-

---

44 I transcribed the vows from a video that is no longer online, which may be found in the Appendix.

45 These events are similar to many others that reformulate definitions of family based on social ties and shared experiences.

46 For example, a woman who kept hitting her thumb when putting up her tent was given the name Smash.

ate only within the local community. The Department of Mutant Vehicles grants permission for vehicles to drive around in Black Rock City but has no standing at all outside the camp. The Black Rock Post Office mails letters from within the camp to the outside world but the use of addresses and stamps is simple and familiar and does not demand any complex interactions. The wedding met the standards outlined on the website so was a legally binding ceremony.[47] No attempt was made to circumvent state and federal laws.[48]

In terms of their attitudes toward the ceremony, the couple critiqued and were sincere at the same time, both mocking weddings ("Let's fucking get this done") and conveying emotions of friendship and love. The ceremony was a means for clarifying their Burning Man worldview and setting up a mechanism to take that worldview into the larger world. If in Black Rock City, "life is bigger and brighter than in the default world and where we may recognize our potential to inhabit the truly extraordinary," participants attempted to convey that message both via their YouTube video and by the continuity of their marriage in the default world.

An alternative version of a wedding at Burning Man is the ritual of Marrying Yourself.[49] As a result of breaking up with her boyfriend and experiencing a general disillusionment about relationships, L. Gabrielle Penabaz decided she did not want to be excluded from the benefits of weddings and marriage (Penabaz 2014). Not having a wedding seemed like one more layer of failure or rejection, so she created a marriage ceremony for herself as a single person. If gay weddings challenge the social norm of a male-female couple, this notion of marriage dispensed with a couple completely, as well as with any issues of the legal role of marriage. This type of wedding appropriated all the supportive and celebratory aspects of weddings, now directed to one person instead of a couple.[50]

The ceremony begins with what Penabaz calls a "zippy exorcism," or divorce from previous, presumably too self–critical, attitudes. The marriage vows are flexible, easily changed to address specific wishes and hopes by filling in blanks on a standard form. Among the possible promises are "Release old images of myself that make me feel unattractive" and "Accept that I am totally responsible for my happiness." The ritual redefines marriage as an emotionally supportive rela-

---

47 At Burning Man, postcards and stamps are gifts and cannot be purchased. The people who supervise the post office and deliver mail in the camps are volunteers.
48 The wedding followed the necessary laws.
49 Penabaz's ceremony (Appendix 1) was developed prior to her participation in Burning Man with the intention of doing it there. She tried it out first in Los Angeles and subsequently performed the rite at two Burning Man festivals (Penabaz 2014, 77).
50 When Penabaz created her ritual in 2012, gay marriage was legal in several states.

tionship. The vow usually said between two people becomes a mode of realigning one's attitude toward oneself. Penabaz writes, "Marrying yourself as an artwork releases the shackles of convention and religion" (Penabaz 2014, 120). Meaninglessness is not invoked here; instead a specific claim is made about the function of art and its role in determining or undermining meaning.

The Marry Yourself rite elicits numerous possible interpretations. All people who undergo the rite must decide for themselves exactly what this type of marriage means, whether they are getting married or participating as the wedding party. During the rites no attempt was made to highlight or negate any interpretations, which not only varied from person to person but also could change during the course of the event. Penabaz's ideas about the artistic and psychological role of marrying yourself are not necessarily adopted by participants.

Marry Yourself rites follow the model of wedding as game and party set forth on the Burning Man website. They can be interpreted as a subversive rejection of normative social patterns even more so than does, for example, gay marriage. Critics of marriage may consider the performance as reinscribing a questionable institution while still others may see this reinscription as a positive appropriation of marriage for those previously excluded. Since the act has no legal consequences, it can also be viewed as pure art.

For both types of weddings, the intense selective attention of ritual permitted participants to depict an idealized world with themselves in it as the events set up models for daily life beyond the wedding (J. Z. Smith 1982). The idealized community, "we are all Burners," included those who attended and participated in the wedding, the larger group of people who had been to Burning Man in the past, those who might simply choose to identify with the group and those who read Penabaz's article.

Mark Auslander argues that rituals have a power of redress since "[r]itual provides highly evocative mechanisms for bringing underlying conundrums into the open in a structured fashion and rendering them, for the most part, manageable and negotiable" (Auslander 2013).[51] One conundrum Burning Man weddings solve is offering a setting for life-cycle events for those who are excluded from or choose to exclude themselves from traditional venues.[52] Burning Man offers a large and vibrant canvas for any and all rite-of-passage events, guaran-

---

51 The particular conundrums that interest Auslander (2013) are related to conflicts between, for example, the work ethic of capitalism and an emphasis on the family.
52 Hoesly discusses the small number of studies on the search for more options to mark events outside traditional venues (Hoesly 2015, 8). On this point, Sarah Pike states, "Death rites at the Mausoleum transformed private grief and loss into public expression in ways that are generally unavailable to most contemporary Americans" (Pike 2005, 198).

teeing a level of excitement and interaction not found easily in daily life. Every type of wedding fits the site, as does every type of mourning.

Weddings, as Mark Auslander notes, can help solve social conflicts around group membership (Auslander 2013). Marrying Yourself includes even single people in the category "married," overcoming what some see as social stigma (e. g., old maid). Each wedding solves the modern dilemma of fractured families by creating as a family group all Burners (current and past). The festival provides a wildly flexible concept of extended family to witness and support the event, with few critical remarks being made despite the number and the variety of people who attend. Family, now defined in a new form, is reidealized in the course of the ceremonies.

Rituals work because they are understood to be specific examples (tokens) of a general type of socially-recognized action. Just as anything can be art at Burning Man, a wide berth of interpretive models connects token to type in Black Rock City. Leeds-Hurwitz argues that most people do not understand the meaning of symbols in the hybrid weddings she studied (2002, 175). Participants are simply not familiar with the traditions. Participants at Burning Man solve this problem by giving everyone the right to make up their own meanings. Indeed any interpretation must be from the participant, including the claim that something is meaningless.

The Psychological Efficacy of Burning Man Rituals

The psychological effects of participation in Burning Man mirror those of rituals in general. Rituals permit individuals to "discover novel aspects of ourselves ... out of such glimpses that we may fabricate meaningful trajectories of self and collectivity" (Auslander 2013). In additional, Burning Man is, in psychoanalytic terms, a "transitional space" (Winnicott 1953).[53] This notion of space, originally described by the pediatrician Donald Winnicott, nurtures creativity because it is less determined, defined, and psychically organized than the realms in which daily life is carried out. In the transitional space, the mother acts so as to permit "the infant the illusion that what the infant creates really exists" (Winnicott

---

53 Winnicott draws attention to "an intermediate area of experiencing, to which inner reality and external life both contribute. It is an area which is not challenged, because no claim is made on its behalf except that it shall exist as a resting-place for the individual engaged in the perpetual human task of keeping inner and outer reality separate yet inter-related" (Winnicott 1953, 90).

1971). This transitional space is then rediscovered in specific adult situations where illusions are permitted and even nurtured, as for example at Burning Man:

Should an adult make claims on us for our acceptance of the objectivity of his subjective phenomena we discern or diagnose madness. If, however, the adult can manage to enjoy the personal intermediate area without making claims, then we can acknowledge our own corresponding intermediate areas, and are pleased to find overlapping, that is to say common experience between members of a group in art or religion or philosophy. (Winnicott 1953, 96)

Transitional spaces offer relief from the continuous demands of reality and the continuous need to match inner and outer reality. "Relief from this strain is provided by an intermediate area of experience," Winnicott explains, "which is not challenged (arts, religion, etc.). This intermediate area is in direct continuity with the play area of the small child who is 'lost' in play" (Winnicott 1953, 96).

Burning Man participants, like a mother-child dyad, share in an illusionary world. The illusionary world is far extended beyond a single dyad. The rites reinforce this illusionary world with an amazing willingness on the part of a huge crowd to join in supporting individual illusions of all types, not all of which may turn out to be positive: "We can share a respect for illusory experience, and if we wish we may collect together and form a group on the basis of the similarity of our illusory experiences. This is a natural root of grouping among human beings" (Winnicott 1953, 90).

Marrying Yourself rituals are extremely interesting examples of transitional-space rites since they permit the participants to imagine new relationships with themselves that are grounded in the larger worldview of the community and thus reinforced. Each event constitutes a similar transitional space with "intense experiencing" or creativity as the "doing that arises out of being" (Winnicott 1971, 39). Black Rock City is a real mirage and a mirage of reality at the same time. Standard clothing can be interpreted as a costume and costumes are standard, confusing the notions of costume and regular clothing.

The crucial difference in this use of Winnicott and the ones critiqued above is that the rites do not function only at the level of play and art-making.[54] The illusionary world of Burning Man is at the same time a functional world both in terms of the context-related aspects of rituals and the concrete goals of making a functional city. That is, while play is part of the event, it takes place as part of socially recognizable and highly consequential actions. The capacity to create and make Black Rock City operative is far beyond the capacity of a child and more tightly entwined with daily life and survival than much artistic expression.

---

54 See the Introduction, page 11.

Unlike in child's play, in the case of Burning Man an entire city is constructed, operates for a week, and then is dismantled. Hundreds of dwellings are built; mail is sent and delivered; individuals with a variety of training deal with illnesses and mediate serious conflicts; cars are registered and are refused registration.[55] Illusion and reality meet in an unexpected way throughout all aspects of the operation of the city. Any form of a wedding ceremony, along with the payment of sixty dollars to the county clerk, results in a legally binding wedding.

The rituals also have multiple levels of efficacy, to enact transformations that are carefully represented both formally and spatially. Every ritual presents a map of the transformation that is presupposed even as it is enacted in that specific instance. It is not the performative speech acts that force this transformation but the taking up of roles (priest who pronounces the formula, couple who is wed) that are socially recognizable based on a shared cosmology (even at Burning Man). As Silverstein explains, "every ritual works the same way, by dynamic figuration that mobilizes participants to role inheritance by particular rule of recruitment, that enacts motion or movement in space and time across multiple semiotic channels, including especially the verbal channel, and that in effect diagrammatically portrays the sought-after transformative goal or end of the event" (Silverstein 2016, 20).

Participants at Burning Man who claim the term "spirituality" ignore religious practitioners who see their own practices as equally spiritual. Burning Man rituals are explicitly constructed in order to carve out a social space that is not connected with traditional religions or their institutions. Gilmore argues that participants exhibit "a much greater awareness of interpretive plasticity" (Gilmore 2010, 69). Participants evince a suspicion about the capacity of words to explain Burning Man, an ideology built around a notion of pure experience. The theme of divine ineffability has been adopted at Burning Man and converted to a theory that locates reality in hard-to-define personal experiences. In this modern setting, the ineffable as "what cannot be spoken about" shifts focus from divinity to the self, the locus of modern experience. Burning Man ideology draws on a popular version of this privileging of experience used in other settings—for example, as a mode of finding the truth in religious experiences. It is possible to strip away language (and thereby representation) and reveal pure experience. In this view experience trumps meaning. "'Meaning' is dog meat in the face of experiment and experience" is how Erik Davis sums up this semiotic ideology (E. Davis 1995). The trace of ashes left by the Burn is said to mean *Here the Man Was Burned*, an action inherently beyond explica-

---

55 As noted above, Black Rock City is the third-largest city in Nevada when it is in operation.

tion.[56] Despite this explicit ideology, life at Burning Man is still full of acts of interpretation, with indeterminate meaning demanding just as much, and perhaps even more, words of explanation.

---

[56] The Man Burn can be understood to exemplify Krauss's (1977a, 75) modern-art "imposition of things."

Conclusions

Ritual is the purest expression of cultural control.
(G. Urban 1991, 112)

Acts of interpretation create culture. They map and clarify for everyone the contextual-linkages and forms of forces that shape daily life, be they gods or bodily pains. Analysis begins with the ideas sign-users employ to support their interpretations and to attack other people's investments. Tracking their explicit statements and debates gives us insight into social practices. The give and take of rhetorical combat about meaning, however, does not easily translate into abstract theory. Peircean terminology, despite being complicated, offers the "gold standard" for distinguishing between types of signs and their social uses (Yelle 2016, 243). Each chapter above elucidates some aspects of these claims, whether it is the limitations of raiding idiosyncratic linguistic models for abstract theory or the Peircean-based insights that might confound sign-users but offer better strategies for comparison.

Reviewing from the first chapter, it is a fascinating question why and how some entity or experience is imagined to be at the limits of language. Reality may be thought to evade the normal functions of language, or to be best represented by some specific linguistic form. Analysis of ancient ideas about ineffability clarifies various, and often contradictory modern reworkings of the concept. Where the deity was once thought to exist in a realm beyond even the best words, currently notions of self are understood to be at the same time ineffable and demanding of (someone specific's) extensive discourse. In some contemporary discourse, the negation of naming is presented as the core of ineffability and therefore central to everything from performance to ethics. Upping the ante, the "negation of negation" is said to transcend the limits of the self, or anything else thought to have boundaries. A close connection is drawn between this elusive self and the privileged realm of personal experience, as linguistic models supply a framework for reality far beyond what speakers are aware of.

In the ancient world, a specific linguistic model of naming was used to motivate all the requisite definitions and equations of what the deity was and was not. Naming was thought to delineate how words turn into deeds as the power of divine names supplied the basis for context-influencing sign-use. Ideas about divine names offered very nuanced models. Discussing the Deuteronomic statement that the deity's name dwells in the Temple, Guy Stroumsa writes, "There is here the beginning of a duality in the divinity, as if God's name was his representative upon earth" (Stroumsa 2005, 186). God's name is always a represen-

https://doi.org/10.1515/9783110768602-008

tation of him; the question is, what kind of representation? The implication of the theology is not that the deity has left *only* his name in the building but instead that the building is very closely associated with him.

Name ideologies have staying power. The post-Platonic debate still toggles between a natural and a conventional basis for names. The natural name of the deity is inherently elusive and powerful, two sides of the same coin. In Philo's case, the very notion of divine names could be used in multiple ways to make subtle and often confusing points about the divine presence in the mundane world. Instead of being beyond language, for Philo divine names must be talked about from many angles in order for a new divine mediation to emerge.

Modern speech-act theory and divine naming offer partial windows into the multifunctionality of language. They differ as to how language uses are plumbed in search of context-relating social efficacy. The contagion of the rigid connection of a name to an object is harder to contain than the efficacy of a conventional speech act, easily dethroned by a mere shift in the verbal form. Both ideologies capture something speakers sense about the power of language: the capacity of names to invoke a presence and of self-reflexive verbs to describe the very action that they enact.

One person's formal divine representation is another person's idol. Richard Davis notes that language often supplies the models used in debates about representation (2001, 121). Once again, no single historical framework for defining and evaluating images can be decontextualized into an abstract definition of correct/incorrect use of images. At stake is the efficacy not only of words but of all sorts of signs understood to stand for divinity. Every religious ritual includes some mediated representation of divinity. Explicit debates seek to determine what constitutes an image and whether or not it is permitted, a process inherently open to reinterpretation.

Authorities attempt to regulate representation by benign and less benign means. Claims depend on either shared discourse that convinces others or the power to enforce norms. Evaluative categories forged in ancient polemics are dusted off and used as neutral descriptions. Brute-force political power is often disguised or simply lost to history as the rhetorical claims pass from one text to another, from one historical context to another. Idolatry is therefore always a retrodetermination in which someone's mode of representation is *post factum* resignified as lacking legitimacy. The shadows of these interventions continue to distort contemporary analysis. Since worship of Yahweh's consort Asherah is condemned by some strands of ancient theology and any humanoid depiction of Yahweh seems to contradict biblical injunctions against divine images, only the most explicitly indexical ancient evidence will be clear enough to counter this interpretative frame.

Yet another model from language was made famous by its inclusion in Paul's letters. With his comparison of letter and spirit, Paul endows linguistic forms with qualities. These qualities seem to be the natural state of those linguistic units. Spirit becomes inextricably connected to heartfelt prayer whereas letters are relegated to the world of flesh and meaningless action.

As Webb Keane warns us, the Protestant attempt to use these models to dematerialize ritual will fail (2007). This study bolsters his argument, supplying evidence from much earlier historical settings. It is at our peril that we ignore why and how the qualities associated with various linguistic forms, as Susan Gal argues (2013, 45), "require us to attend to the justification, explanation, and motivation of action through semiotic processes that reproduce frameworks for 'finding' qualia, thereby bestowing value on everyday material object, including speech." For Paul, though he would not have been able to put the argument in this form, the representational capacity of the material letter is separable from, and inferior to, the intentional meaning of a word. The resulting hierarchy is extremely flexible at giving moral value to some signs at the expense of others.

In the case of ascent liturgies, semiotic analysis is more precise than claims about individual experience. Ascent to the heavens was not dependent on a trance or any other form of altered mental state. Those who used ancient ascent texts interpreted the signs as having contextual implications of the most profound manner, as is true of so many religious texts. The liturgies permitted the liturgists to attain a variety of ritual goals, some directly involved with implicating themselves into the heavenly cult and others what we might call secondary applications of the ritual powers.

Far from being an altered mental state, the presentation of the heavenly sacrificial cult in the *Sabbath Songs* is a beguiling priestly fantasy of sacrifice, once more entextualizing (encapsulating in a text) the already-entextualized sacrifice descriptions found in the Priestly source. In the heavenly cult, all the nonpriestly elements of sacrifice have been eliminated from the picture. The entire cult takes place in an area restricted to priests and involves only priests, from start to finish. The actions of the heavenly cult include blessing, reciting psalms, offering praise, actions that are all presented self-reflexively since are the core of the cultic practices. The earthly version of sacrifice as presented by the Priestly source in its entextualized form does not include any liturgy. Similarly, in the *Sabbath Songs,* sacrifice is presented without any specific citations of liturgy even if the cult is entirely liturgical. The modern analytic crux is not to question whether the rite consisted of words or deeds but articulating the representational ideas by which words represent deeds that are themselves words.

As demonstrated in the analysis of rituals at Burning Man, the term "spiritual" is adopted by participants who want to distance themselves from institutions they eye with suspicion. The focusing lens of Burning Man, what critics might call its version of being an institution, presents a potent mode of flexible interpretation.

Burning Man events employ the stark desert location, music, dance, and costumes to mobilize a broad sweep of senses, emotions, and psychic states. More than one transformation may occur at the same time (psychic, sociological, legal). The power of ritual leads to the creation of a new context (e. g., a married couple whose union has been witnessed by a family-and-friends group) and new modes of expression that can offer participants an array of social and psychological implications. The successful completion of a wedding may coincide with the psychic transformation of participants as well as the very concrete forging of a new socially recognized unit (married couple).

Every participant becomes both an artist and an art critic, explicating to whatever extent they want the meaning of their actions and everything going on around them. The contextual relationships of modern art enacted within the structure of rituals is inseparable from the semiotic opening-up of new possible interpretations even as those signs forge new bonds between someone and another Burner or to themselves. Burning Man rites offer important lessons in ritual elasticity. Rituals may not work or may follow expected lines, but officiants may not be able to control all the meanings of any event even if they want to; the social power unleashed can be hijacked given the semiotic opening-up of new possible interpretations. At Burning Man this elasticity is pushed by participants who have little commitment to following pre-set modes of interpretation, even with the Ten Principles.

Looking back at these examples we can see a basic tension between the stability claimed for religion and the instability of sign meaning. As Keane warns us, "... signs in the human world are inherently contestable and subject to historical transformation" (2018, 83). The relationship between a sign and its object can be altered by a new interpretant. Every sign is ready and waiting for that new interpretation, for an act of interpretation that sets everything in play. This study does not address the elaborate means religious authorities use to control and reinforce permitted interpretations, but readers can imagine just how necessary these forces are. The regimenting forces rely on ideologies and linguistic models to do their work and modern analysts draw, sometimes unwittingly, on this regimentation.

Religious rituals are dependent on signs that are understood to stand for divinity. This "standing for" relationship is formal, so as to give followers vital information about the deity, but it reassures participants that deities are also present. A deity is never beyond representation, even if the very mode of representation is self-reflexively critical of its own capacity to fully represent a deity. Once a sign, even a sign of absence, stands for divinity, condemnations and disagreements will begin. Words and objects may pose issues of materiality with charges of overvaluation. Some listeners and viewers are likely to attribute formal representation where others saw indications of co-occurrence. If there is stability to religious traditions, it comes via a constant retrodetermination of prior interpretations as correct and proper or heretical and empty. These attempts to give fixity to a fluid world lay down such powerful tracks for interpretation. Rituals do a great deal of work organizing meanings. Whether a ritual will reinforce a tradition of interpretation or turn an old meaning on its head is itself another act of interpretation.

Appendix 1: Ninja and Tijuana Vows

Walk down the aisle with music.

Hello everybody tonight as the sun sets on the playa (some time ago), we are gathered here to celebrate the marriage of Tijuana and Ninja so that they may flourish here and in the default world, as husband and wife, as parents to Juliet and Eliot, and of course to their plethora of furry children.

By choosing to commemorate this commitment here at Burning Man, they're sealing their vows before all of us, as witnesses in the place where they first met and where they fell in love.

The playa is a heterotopia. A place of otherness. Where life is bigger and brighter than in the default world and where we may recognize our potential to inhabit the truly extraordinary.

Some of you have known these two for years. Many have just met them, but the thing that we all have in common is that we are burners.

Whether this is your first time on the playa, or you've been coming here for decades, you have proven yourselves by your presence here to be extraordinary people who want to make life... make meaning out of life in radical and unique ways.

This is why we are honored to have you here. A community of self-reliant free-thinking individuals to share in the joy in the connection they find with like-minded people.

It is this spirit that creates a new Black Rock city every year

It is this mindset that binds us all from so many different backgrounds together.

Before they exchange vows, Tijuana and Ninja would like to acknowledge those who could not be here: their beloved parents and siblings, Donna and John, Michelle, Jim, Becky, and Laura, all members of camp sausage hang, and moist panties... that's right, who could not burn with us this year. Especially Sassian Player who originally brought them together, and their friends near and far who make life worth living.

And on that note, who gives this woman away in marriage to this man?

I do [not father of the bride]

Excellent. Noted.

The road that brought Tijuana and Ninja together has been full of challenges, but those have strengthened their resolve because they have taken them on together. In honor of their promise to meet all of life's challenges with the same ever-increasing strength, they will now exchange vows. Tijuana?

First of all,

[Photo: you're awesome.]

https://doi.org/10.1515/9783110768602-009

And what's not to get
[Photo: Tijuana and Ninja in front of a barn with child.]
You are the bridge to my every thought
[Photo: Tijuana in front of a bridge.]
The sunshine will tell you so photo: Tijuana and Ninja together smiling.
So, alright
[Photo: "Let's fucking do this" photo of man drinking coffee.]
[Ninja says to all] "I was going to say what it says, it says let's fucking do this.")
[Tijuana whispers] That was just between me and you.
Taz to the Temple Shatzi too Photo: cat
We are off to the Esplanade
For our espionage Photo: The two of them in front of a sign that reads Esplanade
Cause we are all in this together Photo: many shoes
We're keeping this ship afloat photo: of them two
Which brings me home photo: of him in front of a garage with letters on it that read "Welcome home Jeffy"
 We get busy living photo: A man with words "I guess it comes down to a simple choice, really. Get busy living, or get busy dying.
So..Organic smooches Photo: of them kissing
The future is an infinite succession of nows.
Avoid fuzzy thinking and self-deception, your clear vision today will help build a solid foundation. Which will bring us joy Photo: of young girl
For tomorrow. You know, no mistakes just happy accidents. I win (the cute war), Photo: of an elephant. We win.
Blessed dreams ignited. Photo: statue
Imagination. Here. Photo: aerial view of field.
So, let the butterfly land on your nose. Photo: of dog with butterfly
I will show you mine if you show me yours. Photo: cartoon with stick figures.
So now we are home, you, me, and the blinky ball. Photo: pink spiky ball on dashboard
A new journey, man. Our journey. Photo: side of road.
a journey of travel patience Photo: Tijuana standing in traffic
dealing with the shit!
Photo: porta potties.
crazy shit! Photo: Tijuana wearing goggles
Ninja: (inaudible)... Porta potties
Knowing happiness is not a destination but a way in which we travel photo: hills
Reaching home... I lost my place... Reaching home Photo: of burning man
And making beautiful new friends. Photos: Tijuana with friends
I need to know- will you help tie this knot? Photo: of a knot

Seriously? Like seriously, see the heart?

These are my vows. Photo: screenshot of text message

Officiant: Ninja?

Ninja: This is really exciting

Tijuana: ... photo: paper reading Tijuana and Ninja Burning man 2013 Cargo Cult

Now it's our journey man...

Tijuana: I apologize you guys couldn't see those (the photos). I tried to set it up...

Ninja: We'll show you later

Tijuana: before we found each other, I did not fully understand what it means to love and be loved.

It took me 39 years to find you in this life.

But I am certain we have known each other from time out of mind.

Words are, and have always allegedly been my gift.

I am a writer. I am a professor and an ABD doctor of philosophy, and yet when I try and find the words to express how I feel about you, I can't seem to make them connect in a way that's at all worthy.

I've tried so many times to craft some sort of poetic testament of what you mean to me and I just keep coming up short.

Ours is such a perfectly postmodern relationship.

We met at Burning Man. Our early courtship was long distance. We Facebooked, we skyped, and our desire for connection.

And you flew up to Davis at every possible opportunity to fulfill our desire for closeness.

We forged a thriving family with my daughters. Now, our girls.

Juliet and Eli. Through beautiful and transient moments. You are my family, and in the absence of adequate poetry or song that even hints at my love for you, I thought I would make a list of some of the reasons I want to be your wife. That's how I roll.

Tijuana: You love this.

Ninja: You make me feel safe

You make me feel strong even in my weakest moments

You are my last thought when I fall asleep and my first thought when I wake

You turn even the most ordinary days into the most extraordinary gifts

You make me want to be a better person

You are open and honest always

You have the biggest heart of anyone I've ever known

You make me laugh until I literally can't breathe

I'm blown away by your capacity to engage intelligently and critically with the world around you

You've welcomed and made me feel a part of your amazing family and you've become a part of mine

And above all, oh fuck... (cries) you've earned the unconditional love of the two most precious people on the planet.

Juliet and Eliot have been moping and missing you ever since you left on Sunday. I had to deal with that, Thank you.

I can't believe my luck in finding such a wonderful partner.

You see me with your heart, I see you with mine.

Here at burning man, the place that we met, our home, I promise I will always do my utmost to make you happy and (inaudible) to deserve the happiness that you give me.

Officiant: whoo, I got to follow that. Now as a symbol of the vows they have just made, Tijuana and Ninja will exchange burning man 2013 dog tags.

Tijuana, please repeat these words after me:

I give you this tag as a symbol of our love (Tijuana repeats)

For yesterday, today, and tomorrow, and all the days to come (Tijuana repeats)

Wear it as a sign of what we promised (Tijuana repeats)

And know that my love is present, even when I am not (Tijuana repeats)

All right Ninja, your turn.

Ninja, please repeat these words.

I give you this tag as a symbol of our love (Ninja repeats)

For yesterday, today, and tomorrow, and all the days to come (Ninja repeats)

Wear it as a sign of what we promised (Ninja repeats)

And know that my love is present, even when I am not (Ninja repeats)

Ninja: Thank you

Officiant: Tijuana, do you take Ninja to be your wife, to be equal and devoted partners as long as you both shall live?

Tijuana: (inaudible)

Officiant: Ninja, do you take Tijuana to be your husband, to be equal and devoted partners as long as you both shall live?

Ninja: Yes, I do.

Officiant: Well no marriage can survive without the support of community. So, does everyone here pledge to do everything that they possibly can to love and support and make sure that this couple is successful?

(cheers)

Alright, let's bring out that champagne first. Where's the champagne?

We do the champagne first, yes?

Anyway, alright, champagne later, kiss first.

By the faith you have vested in me, I know pronounce you husband and wife. You may now...Ladies and gentlemen, the bride and groom.

(gets champagne) Here we go.

(some Hebrew)

(glass wrapped in napkin to be smashed placed on ground)

Tijuana: do you want this side?

Ninja: I'll take this side.

(both smash glass)

(many mazel tovs from crowd)

(chatter)

Appendix 2: Marry Yourself Vows

Taken from Penabaz (2014, 125)

Til Death Do You Part – Marry Yourself!   www.EncouragingPriestess.com

VOWS

Blanks are for you to fill in as you wish. Use the back of this page if you need.
Do you have any vows you would like to use? Write them down. What's important to you?
What would you like the Priestess to guide you through? Is there any feeling you would like to ritualize?

PLEASE CHECK OR WRITE 5 VOWS TOTAL

You may begin with a Quick Emotional Cleanse, – (AKA- Zippy Exorcism or "Divorce" from old selves)
List things you would like to release here:_____

I promise to:

Forgive Myself
Never deceive myself
Release old images of myself that make me feel unattractive
Accept that I can make serious mistakes and be downright human
Never Cast or Curse on Myself (Even in those little moments when you call yourself "stupid" or "clumsy")
Love Myself like I love those whom I most treasure
Know my Genius and Do Things to Remind Myself of It
Cherish My Strange Wonder
Obey My Small Voice That Knows The Truth and What's Right
Do the Right Thing so I can live with myself in peace
Find Myself Gorgeous and Mysterious When I Need That Boost and Nobody is Around
Kick my own ass when I need it and not expect others to do it for me

https://doi.org/10.1515/9783110768602-010

Expect the best from myself – in spite of any old voices (parents/teachers/etc) who tell me different
Feel wealthy and be generous with my resources even when I feel broke
Understand my own signals for when I need help – and get the help I need
I will fix imbalances instead of accepting blindly or flipping out
Rethink my situation *(ex: values, jobs, and relationships)* when my identity is at stake
I will release my pain on a regular basis through (add word: ex. writing, crying)
Evaluate what is important and embrace the outcome. Life is short.
Accept that I am totally responsible for my own happiness.
I will take steps on a regular basis to achieve harmony around me.
Bring sweetness into my life even when it seems far-fetched.

After today, you may want to create wedding rituals on your own.
Some suggestions to keep the flame alive:
Gifts to yourself that remind you of your vows. Find a proper place to put them so they serve as reminders.
Something to wear every day is good – rings are the norm, but even a perfume can remind you of your vows.
Something to read – inspiring quote or something you have written.
A list of things to release and things to bring into your life. A thing to taste to heighten the sense of the moment.
A closing statement to solidify the ritual.

The House of St. Eve   www.TheSaintEve.com

Vows

Bibliography

Ackerman, Susan. 1992. *Under Every Green Tree: Popular Religion in Sixth-Century Judah*. Harvard Semitic Monographs 46. Atlanta: Scholars Press.

Ahbel-Rappe, Sara. 2000. *Reading Neoplatonism: Non-Discursive Thinking in the Texts of Plotinus, Proclus, and Damascius*. Cambridge, U.K.; New York: Cambridge University Press.

Alexander, Philip S. 2006. *Companion to the Qumran Scrolls: Mystical Texts*. Library of Second Temple Studies. London: T&T Clark.

Althusser, Louis. 1994. "Ideology and Ideological State Apparatus (Notes Towards an Investigation)." In *Mapping Ideology*, edited by Slavoj Žižek, 100–140. London: Verso.

Anderson, Gary. 2009. *Sin: A History*. New Haven: Yale University Press.

Asad, Talal. 1993. Genealogies of Religion: Discipline and Reasons of Power in Christianity and Islam. Baltimore and London: Johns Hopkins University Press.

Assmann, Jan. 1997. Moses the Egyptian : The Memory of Egypt in Western Monotheism. Cambridge: Harvard University Press.

Auslander, Mark. 2013. "How Families Work: Love, Labor and Mediated Oppositions in American Domestic Ritual." In *Applying Cultural Anthropology: An Introductory Reader*, edited by Aaron Podolefsky, Peter Brown, and Scott Lacy, 46–63. Boston: McGraw Hill.

Austin, John L. 1962. *How to Do Things with Words*. Oxford: Clarendon Press.

Baden, Joel S. 2012. The Composition of the Pentateuch: Renewing the Documentary Hypothesis. New Haven: Yale University Press.

Bakhtin, Mikhail M., and Michael Holquist. 1981. *The Dialogic Imagination: Four Essays*. University of Texas Press Slavic Series, no 1. Austin: University of Texas Press.

Ball, Christopher. 2014. "On Dicentization." *Journal of Linguistic Anthropology* 24: 151–173.

Barasch, Moshe. 1992. *Icon : Studies in the History of an Idea*. New York: New York University Press.

Barney, Rachel. 1997. "Plato on Conventionalism." *Phronesis* 42: 143–162.

Basso, Ellen B. 1987. In Favor of Deceit : A Study of Tricksters in an Amazonian Society. Tucson: University of Arizona Press.

Bauman, Richard, and Charles Briggs. 1990. "Poetics and Performance as Critical Perspectives on Language and Social Life." *Annual Review of Anthropology* 19: 59–88.

Baxter, Timothy. 1992. *The Cratylus: Plato's Theory of Naming*. Leiden: Brill.

Bell, Catherine. 1998. "Performance." In *Critical Terms for Religious Studies*, edited by Mark C. Taylor, 205–224. Chicago: University of Chicago Press.

Belting, Hans. 1994. Likeness and Presence: A History of the Image before the Era of Art. Chicago: University of Chicago Press.

Benjamin, Walter. 1968. "The Work of Art in the Age of Mechanical Reproduction." In *Illuminations*, 214–218. London: Fontana.

Berlejung, Angelika. 1997. "Washing the Mouth: The Consecration of Divine Images in Mesopotamia." In *The Image and the Book: Iconic Cults, Aniconism, and the Rise of Book Religion in Israel and the Ancient Near East*, edited by Karel van der Toorn, 45–72. Leuven: Uitgeverij Peeters.

Bertini, Daniele. 2007. "The Transcendence of Sophia in Plotinus' Treatise on Intelligible Beauty." In *Metaphysical Patterns in Platonism*, edited by John F. Finamore and Robert M. Berchman, 33–44. New Orleans: University of the South.

https://doi.org/10.1515/9783110768602-011

Bickerman, Elias J., and Morton Smith. 1976. *The Ancient History of Western Civilization.* New York: Harper and Row.

Blowers, Paul M. 2012. Drama of the Divine Economy: Creator and Creation in Early Christian Theology and Piety. 1st ed. Oxford: Oxford University Press.

Bohak, Gideon. 2003. "The Ibis and the Jewish Question: Ancient 'Anti-Semitism' in Historical Perspective." In *Jews and Gentiles in the Holy Land in the Days of the Second Temple, the Mishnah and the Talmud,* edited by Menahen Mor, Aharon Oppenheimer, Jack Pastor, and Daniel Schwartz, 27–43. Jerusalem: Yad Ben-Zvi.

Bourdieu, Pierre. 1990. *The Logic of Practice.* Stanford: Stanford University Press.

Boustan, Ra'anan. 2004. "Angels in the Architecture: Temple Art and the Poetics of Praise in the Songs of the Sabbath Sacrifice." In *Heavenly Realms and Earthly Realities in Late Antique Religions,* 195–212. Cambridge: Cambridge University Press.

Boustan, Ra'anan, Martha Himmelfarb, and Peter Schäfer, eds. 2013. *Hekhalot Literature in Context: Between Byzantium and Babylonia.* Texte Und Studien Zum Antiken Judentum, 153. Tübingen: Mohr Siebeck.

Bowditch, Rachel. 2010. On The Edge of Utopia: Performance and Ritual at Burning Man. London: Seagull Books.

Boyarin, Daniel. 1994. *A Radical Jew: Paul and the Politics of Identity.* Berkeley: University of California Press.

Bremmer, Jan. 2008. "Iconoclast, Iconoclastic, and Iconoclasm: Notes Towards a Genealogy." *Church History and Religious Culture* 88: 1–17.

Brown, Peter. 1971. "The Rise and Function of the Holy Man in Late Antiquity." *Journal of Roman Studies* 61: 80–101.

Brown, Peter. 1982. *Society and the Holy in Late Antiquity.* Berkeley: University of California Press.

Burning Man. 2021. Playa Weddings. https://burningman.org/event/preparation/playa-living/weddings/. Accessed June 20, 2021.

Bussanich, John. 2007. "Plotinus on the Being of the One." In *Metaphysical Patterns in Platonism,* edited by John F. Finamore and Robert M. Berchman, 57–71. New Orleans: University of the South.

Butler, Judith. 1997a. Excitable Speech : A Politics of the Performative. New York: Routledge.

Butler, Judith. 1997b. *The Psychic Life of Power: Theories in Subjection.* Stanford: Stanford University Press.

Canetti, Elias. 1962. *Crowds and Power.* London: Gollancz.

Carter, Jeffrey. 2003. *Understanding Religious Sacrifice: A Reader.* London: Continuum.

Chazon, Esther. 2000. "Liturgical Communion with the Angels at Qumran." In *Sapiential, Liturgical and Poetic Texts from Qumran,* edited by Daniel Falk, F. García Martínez, and Eileen Schuller, 95–105. Leiden: Brill.

Chazon, Esther. 2003. "Human and Angelic Prayer in Light of the Dead Sea Scrolls." In *Liturgical Perspectives: Prayer and Poetry in Light of the Dead Sea Scrolls,* edited by Esther Chazon, Ruth Clements, and Avital Pinnick, 35–47. Leiden: Brill.

Chidester, David. 1992. *Word and Light : Seeing, Hearing, and Religious Discourse.* Urbana: University of Illinois Press.

Clooney, Francis. 1985. "Sacrifice and Its Spiritualization in the Christian and Hindu Traditions: A Study in Comparative Theology." *Harvard Theological Review* 78: 361–380.

Clupper, Wendy. 2007. "The Performance Culture of Burning Man." Ph.D. Thesis. College Park: University of Maryland.

CNN. 2009. Obama retakes oath of office after Roberts' mistake. https://www.cnn.com/2009/POLITICS/01/21/obama.oath/index.html (accessed June 20, 2021).

Curtis, Edward. 1992. "Idolatry." In *Anchor Dictionary of the Bible*, edited by David Noel Freidman, 3:376 – 381. New York: Doubleday.

Dan, Joseph. 1995. "The Book of the Divine Name by Rabbi Eleazer of Worms." *Frankfurter Judaistische Beiträge* 22: 27 – 60.

Danto, Arthur. 1986. *The Philosophical Disenfranchisement of Art*. New York: Columbia University Press.

Danto, Arthur. 1998. "The End of Art: A Philosophical Defense." *History and Theory* 37: 127 – 143.

Davila, James. 1993. "Prolegomena to a Critical Edition of the Hekhalot Rabbati." *Journal of Jewish Studies*, 208 – 225.

Davila, James. 2000. Eerdsmans Commentaries on the Dead Sea Scrolls: Liturgical Words. Grand Rapids: Eerdmans.

Davila, James. 2001. Descenders to the Chariot: The People Behind the Hekhalot Literature. Boston: Leiden.

Davila, James. 2013. Hekhalot Literature in Translation: Major Texts of Merkavah Mysticism. Leiden: Brill.

Davis, Erik. 1995. "Terminal Beach Party: Warming up to the Burning Man Festival." *Village Voice*, October 31, 1995.

Davis, Richard. 2001. "Indian Image-Worship and Its Discontents." In *Representation in Religion: Studies in Honor of Moshe Barash*, edited by Jan Assmann and Albert Baumgarten, 107 – 132. Leiden: Brill.

Dick, Michael. 1999. "Prophetic Parodies of Making the Cult Image." In *Born in Heaven, Made on Earth: The Making of the Cult Image in the Ancient Near East*, edited by Michael Dick, 1 – 53. Winona Lake: Eisenbrauns.

Dick, Michael. 2005. "The Mesopotamian Cult Statue: A Sacramental Encounter with Divinity." In *Cult Image and Divine Representation in the Ancient Near East*, edited by Neal H. Walls, 43 – 67. Boston: American Schools of Oriental Research.

Diez Macho, Alejandro. 1968. Neophyti 1. Targum Palestiniense Ms de La Biblioteca Vaticana. Madrid: CSIC.

Dillon, John. 1977. *The Middle Platonists 80 B.C. to A.D. 220*. Ithaca: Cornell University Press.

Dillon, John. 1996. "Damascius on the Ineffable." *Archiv für Geschichte Der Philosophie* 78: 120 – 129.

Dillon, John. 1999. "Monotheism in the Gnostic Tradition." In *Pagan Monotheism in Late Antiquity*, edited by Polymnia Athanassiadi and Michael Frede, 69 – 79. Oxford: Clarendon Press.

Dillon, John. 2002. "The Platonic Philosopher at Prayer." In *Metaphysik Und Religion: Zur Singatur Des Spåtantiken Denkens*, edited by Theo Kobusch and Michael Erler, 279 – 295. München: K.G. Saur.

Dorrie, Heinrich. 1944. "Der Platoniker Eudoros von Alexandria." *Hermes: Zeitschrift für Klassische Philologie* 79: 25 – 38.

Durkheim, Emile. 2001. *The Elementary Forms of Religious Life.* Edited by Mark Sydney Cladis. Translated by Carol Cosman. Oxford World's Classics. Oxford; New York: Oxford University Press.

Dyer, George. 2001. "Review of The Desert." *The Guardian*, February 24, 2001.

Ehrenkrook, Jason von. 2008. "Sculpture, Space and the Poetics of Idolatry in Josephus' Bellum Judaicum." *Journal for the Study of Judaism* 39: 170–191.

Ehrenkrook, Jason von. 2011. Sculpting Idolatry in Flavian Rome: (An)Iconic Rhetoric in the Writings of Flavius Josephus. Atlanta: Society of Biblical Literature.

Ellenbogen, Josh, and Aaron Tugendhaft. 2011. *Idol Anxiety.* Stanford: Stanford University Press.

Elsner, Jas. 2007. *Roman Eyes: Visuality & Subjectivity in Art & Text.* Princeton: Princeton University Press.

Fine, Steven. 2005a. *Art and Judaism in the Greco-Roman World: Toward a New Jewish Archaeology.* Cambridge, U.K.; New York: Cambridge University Press.

Fine, Steven. 2005b. "Liturgy and the Art of the Dura Europos Synagogue." In *Liturgy in the Life of the Synagogue: Studies in the History of Jewish Prayer*, edited by Ruth Langer and Steven Fine, 41–71. Winona Lake: Eisenbrauns.

Fine, Steven. 2014. *Art, History, and the Historiography of Judaism in Roman Antiquity.* Brill Reference Library of Judaism, Volume 34.

Fleming, Luke. 2011. "Name Taboos and Rigid Performativity." *Anthropological Quarterly* 84: 141–164.

Fleming, Luke, and Michael Lempert. 2011. "Introduction: Beyond Bad Words." *Anthropological Quarterly* 84: 5–13.

Fleming, Luke, and Michael Lempert. 2014. "Poetics and Performativity." In *Cambridge Handbook of Linguistic Anthropology*, edited by N. J. Enfield, Paul Kockelman, and Jack Sidnell, 485–515. Cambridge: Cambridge University Press.

Fletcher-Louis, Crispin H. T. 2002. *All the Glory of Adam : Liturgical Anthropology in the Dead Sea Scrolls.* Studies on the Texts of the Desert of Judah; v. 42. Leiden; Boston: Brill.

Fortunati, Allegra. 2005. "Utopia, Social Sculpture, and Burning Man." In *AfterBurn: Reflections on Burning Man*, edited by Lee Gilmore and Mark Van Proyen, 151–170. Albuquerque: University of New Mexico Press.

Foucault, Michel, and Jay Miskowiec. 1986. "Of Other Spaces: Utopias and Heterotopias." *Diacritics: A Review of Contemporary Criticism* 16: 22–27.

Frazer, James George. 1947. *The Golden Bough: A Study in Magic and Religion.* New York: Macmillan.

Freedberg, David. 1985. *Iconoclasts and Their Motives.* Gerson Lecture 2nd. Montclair: G. Schwartz.

Freedberg, David. 1996. "Holy Images and Other Images." In *The Art of Interpreting*, edited by Susan C. Scott, 69–80. University Park: Pennsylvania State University Press.

Freedman, Samuel. 2015. "Couples Personalizing Role of Religion in Wedding Ceremonies." *New York Times*, June 26, 2015, sec. On Religion. https://www.nytimes.com/2015/06/27/us/couples-personalizing-role-of-religion-in-wedding-ceremonies.html.

Freud, Sigmund. 1953–1966. Trans. and eds. James Strachey, Anna Freud, Alix Strachey, and Alan Tyson. *The Standard Edition of the Complete Psychological Works of Sigmund Freud.* 24 vols. London: The Hogarth Press and the Institute of Psycho-analysis.

Gal, Susan. 1998. "Multiplicity and Contention among Language Ideologies." In *Language Ideologies: Practice and Theory*, 423–442. Oxford: Oxford University Press.

Gal, Susan. 2013. "Tastes of Talk: Qualia and the Moral Flavor of Signs." *Anthropological Theory* 13: 31–48.

Gamboni, Dario. 1997. The Destruction of Art: Iconoclasm and Vandalism since the French Revolution. Picturing History. London: Reaktion Books.

García Martinez, Florentino, Eibert J. C. Tigchelaar, and Adam S. van der Woude. 1998. "11QShirot 'Olat Ha-Shabbat." In *Qumran Cave 11.II (11Q2–18, 11Q20–31)*. Vol. 23. DJD. Oxford: Clarendon Press.

Gennep, Arnold van. 1960. The Rites of Passage. Chicago: University of Chicago Press.

Gilmore, Lee. 2010. Theater in a Crowded Fire: Ritual and Spirituality at Burning Man. Berkeley: University of California Press.

Goodenough, Erwin Ramsdell, and Jacob Neusner. 1988. *Jewish Symbols in the Greco-Roman Period*. Abridged. Bollingen Series. Princeton: Princeton University Press.

Goodman, Nelson. 1972. "Seven Strictures on Similarity." In *Problems and Projects*, 437–447. Indianapolis and New York: Bobbs-Merrill Company.

Gradel, Ittai. 2002. *Emperor Worship and Roman Religion*. Oxford: Oxford University Press.

Grant, Robert. 1952. Miracle and Natural Law in Graeco-Roman and Early Christian Thought. Amsterdam: North Holland.

Green, Denise Nicole. 2009. "Somewhere in Between: Transformative Spaces, Shifting Masculinities, and Community Style." M.A. Thesis. Davis California: University of California-Davis.

Hägg, Henny Fiskå. 2006. *Clement of Alexandria and the Beginnings of Christian Apophaticism*. Oxford Early Christian Studies. Oxford; New York: Oxford University Press.

Halbertal, Moshe, and Avishai Margalit. 1992. *Idolatry*. Cambridge: Harvard University Press.

Hanks, William. 1989. "Text and Textuality." *Annual Review of Anthropology* 18: 95–127.

Hanson, Anthony. 1967. "Philo's Etymologies." *Journal of Theological Studies* 18: 128–139.

Harren, Natilee. 2016. "Fluxus and the Transitional Commodity." *Art Journal* 75(1): 44–69.

Harvey, Stewart. 2017. *Playa Fire: Spirit and Soul at Burning Man*. San Francisco: HarperElixir.

Hayman, Peter. 1989. "Was God a Magician, Sefer-Yesira and Jewish Magic." *Journal of Jewish Studies* 40(2): 225–237.

Hetherington, Kevin. 1997. *The Badlands of Modernity: Heterotopia and Social Ordering*. International Library of Sociology. London; New York: Routledge.

Himmelfarb, Martha. 1993. *Ascent to Heaven in Jewish and Christian Apocalypses*. New York: Oxford University Press.

Hockett, Jeremy. 2004. "Reckoning Ritual and Counterculture in the Burning Man Community: Communication, Ethnography, and the Self in Reflexive Modernism." Ph.D. Thesis. Albuquerque: University of New Mexico.

Hoesly, Dusty. 2015. "'Need a Minister? How about Your Brother?': The Universal Life Church between Religion and Non-Religion." *Secularism and Nonreligion* 4(12): 1–13.

Hollywood, Amy. 1995. "Review of Michael Sells' The Mystical Languages of Unsaying." *Journal of Religion* 75: 564–565.

Hollywood, Amy. 2002. "Performativity, Citationality, Ritualization." *History of Religions* 42: 93–115.

Hubert, Henri, and Marcel Mauss. 1899. *Sacrifice: Its Nature and Function*. Chicago: University of Chicago Press.

Hundley, Michael. 2009. "To Be or Not To Be: A Re-Examination of Name Language in Deuteronomy and the Deuteronomistic History." *Vetus Testamentum* 59: 533–555.

Hurowitz, Victor. 2012. "What Can Go Wrong with an Idol?" In *Iconoclasm and Text Destruction in the Ancient Near East and Beyond*, edited by Natalie N. May, 259–310. Chicago: University of Chicago.

Huss, Boaz. 2014. "Spirituality: The Emergence of a New Cultural Category and Its Challenge to the Religious and the Secular." *Journal of Contemporary Religion* 29(1): 47–60.

Idel, Moshe. 1981. "The Concept of Torah in Hekhalot Literature and Its Metamorphoses in Kabbalah." *Jerusalem Studies in Jewish Thought* I: 323–384.

Jakobson, Roman. 1960. "Linguistics and Poetics." In *Style in Language*, edited by Thomas Sebeok, 350–377. Cambridge: M.I.T. Press.

Janowitz, Naomi. 1993. "Re-Creating Genesis: The Metapragmatics of Divine Speech." In *Reflexive Language*, edited by John Lucy, 393–405. Cambridge: Cambridge University Press.

Janowitz, Naomi. 1997. "Rabbis and Their Opponents: The Construction of the 'Min' in Rabbinic Anecdotes." *Journal of Early Christian Studies* 6(3): 449–462.

Janowitz, Naomi. 2008. "Good Jews Don't: Historical and Philosophical Constructions of Idolatry." *History of Religions* 47: 59–86.

Johnson, J. Cale. 2013. "Indexical Iconicity in Sumerian Belles Lettres." *Language and Communications* 33: 26–49.

Johnson, J. Cale. 2017. "The Stuff of Causation: Etiological Metaphor and Pathogenic Channeling in Babylonian Medicine." In *The Comparable Body: Imagination and Analogy in Ancient Anatomy and Physiology*, edited by John Z. Wee, 72–122. Leiden: Brill.

Johnston, Sarah. 1997. "Rising to the Occasion: Theurgic Ascent in Its Cultural Milieu." In *Envisioning Magic*, edited by Peter Schaefer and Hans Kippenberg, 165–193. Leiden: Brill.

Jufresa, Montserrat. 1981. "Basilides, A Path to Plotinus." *Vigiliae Christianae: A Review of Early Christian Life and Language* 35: 1–15.

Katz, Steven. 1978. "Language, Epistemology and Mysticism." In *Mysticism and Philosophical Analysis*, edited by Steven Katz, 22–74. Studies in Philosophy and Religion. London: Sheldon Press.

Keane, Webb. 2007. *Christian Moderns: Freedom and Fetish in the Mission Encounter*. Berkeley: University of California Press.

Keane, Webb. 2018. "On Semiotic Ideology." *Signs and Society* 6: 64–87.

Kehoe, Alice Beck. 2000. Shamans and Religion : An Anthropological Exploration in Critical Thinking. Prospect Heights: Waveland Press.

Kendall, Laurel. 1996. "Initiating Performance: The Story of Chini, a Korean Shaman." In *The Performance of Healing*, edited by Carol Laderman and Marina Roseman, 17–58. New York: Routledge.

Kennedy, Charles. 1994. "The Semantic Field of the Term 'Idolatry.'" In *Uncovering Ancient Stones*, edited by Lewis M. Hopfe, 193–204. Winona Lake: Eisenbrauns.

Kennedy, Charles. 1997. Comparative Rhetoric: An Historical and Cross-Cultural Introduction. Oxford: Oxford University Press.

Kimelman, Reuven. 2005. "Blessing Formulae and Divine Sovereignty in Rabbinic Liturgy." In *Liturgy in the Life of the Synagogue: Studies in the History of Jewish Prayer*, edited by Ruth Langer and Steven Fine, 1–39. Winona Lake: Eisenbrauns.

Kirby, Michael, and Jim Dine. 1965. *Happenings*. 1st ed. New York: Dutton.

Kittel, Gerhard, and Gerhard Friedrich, eds. 1964–1976. *Theological Dictionary of the New Testament*. Translated by Geoffrey William Bromiley. 10 vols. Grand Rapids, Mich.: Eerdmans.

Klawans, Jonathan. 2002. "Interpreting the Last Supper: Sacrifice, Spiritualization, and Anti-Sacrifice." *New Testament Studies* 48: 1–17.

Klawans, Jonathan. 2006. Purity, Sacrifice, and the Temple: Symbolism and Supersessionism in the Study of Ancient Judaism. Oxford: Oxford University Press.

Klein, Michael. 1982. Anthropomorphism and Anthropopathisms in the Targumin of the Pentateuch. Jerusalem: Makor.

Kraeling, Carl H. 1979. *The Synagogue*. The Excavations at Dura-Europos Augmented Edition, final report 8, pt 1. New York: Ktav Pub. House.

Krauss, Rosalind. 1977a. "Notes of the Index: Seventies Art in American (Part 1)." *October* 3: 68–81.

Krauss, Rosalind. 1977b. "Notes on the Index: Seventies Art in America (Part 2)." *October* 4: 58–67.

Kretzmann, Norman. 1971. "Plato on the Correctness of Names." *American Philosophical Quarterly* 8: 126–138.

Kripke, Saul. 1980. *Naming and Necessity*. Cambridge: Harvard University Press.

Lakoff, George, and Mark Johnson. 1980. *Metaphors We Live By*. Chicago: University of Chicago Press.

Laplanche, Jean, and Jean-Bertrand Pontalis. 1973. *The Language of Psychoanalysis*. London: Hogarth Press.

Laqueur, Thomas. 1990. *Making Sex: Body and Gender from the Greeks to Freud*. Cambridge: Harvard University Press.

Lawrence, Marilynn. 2007. "Who Thought the Stars Are Causes? The Astrological Doctrine Criticized by Plotinus." In *Metaphysical Patterns in Platonism*, edited by John F. Finamore and Robert M. Berchman, 17–31. University of the South.

Layton, Bentley. 1987. The Gnostic Scriptures: A New Translation with Annotations and Introductions. 1st ed. Garden City: Doubleday.

Layton, Bentley. 1989. "The Significance of Basilides in Ancient Christian Thought." *Representations* 28: 135–151.

Lee, Benjamin. 1997. Talking Heads: Language, Metalanguage, and the Semiotics of Subjectivity. Durham: Duke University Press.

Lee, Benjamin, and Edward LiPuma. 2002. "Cultures of Circulation: The Imaginations of Modernity." *Public Culture: Bulletin of the Society for Transnational Cultural Studies* 14: 191–213.

Leeds-Hurwitz, Wendy. 2002. *Wedding as Text: Communicating Cultural Identities through Ritual*. LEA's Communication Series. Mahwah; London: Lawrence Erlbaum Associates.

Leicht, Reimund. 2013. "Major Trends in Rabbinic Cosmology." In *Hekhalot Literature in Context*, edited by Boustan, Ra'anan, Martha Himmelfarb, and Peter Schäfer, 245–278. Tübingen: Mohr Siebeck.

Lempert, Michael. 2007. "Conspicuously Past: Distressed Discourse and Diagrammatic Embedding in a Tibetan Represented Speech Style." *Language and Communication* 27(3): 258–271.

Leone, Massimo, and Richard Parmentier. 2014. "Representing Transcendence: The Semiosis of Real Presence." *Signs and Society* 2: S1–22.

Levenson, Jon. 1994. Creation and the Persistence of Evil: The Jewish Drama of Divine Omnipotence. Princeton: Princeton University Press.

Levtow, Nathaniel B. 2008. *Images of Others: Iconic Politics in Ancient Israel*. Winona Lake: Eisenbrauns.

Lieber, Andrea. 2007. "Between Motherland and Fatherland: Diaspora, Pilgrimage and the Spiritualization of Sacrifice in Philo of Alexandria." In *Heavenly Tablets: Interpretation, Identity and Tradition in Ancient Judaism*, edited by Lynn LiDonnici and Andrea Lieber, 193–210. Leiden: Brill.

LiPuma, Edward. 2000. *Encompassing Others: The Magic of Modernity in Melanesia*. Ann Arbor: University of Michigan Press.

Litwa, M. David. 2014. "The Deification of Moses in Philo of Alexandria." *The Studia Philonica Annual* 26: 1–27.

Long, Alex. 2008. "Plato's Dialogues and a Common Rationale for Dialogue Form." In *The End of Dialogue in Antiquity*, edited by Simon Goldhill, 45–59. Cambridge: Cambridge University Press.

Lucy, John Arthur. 1992. *Language Diversity and Thought: A Reformulation of the Linguistic Relativity Hypothesis*. Studies in the Social and Cultural Foundations of Language, no. 12. Cambridge; New York: Cambridge University Press.

Mack, Burton. 1987. "Introduction: Religion and Ritual." In *Violent Origins: Walter Burkert, René Girard, and Jonathan Z. Smith on Ritual Killing and Cultural Formation*, edited by Robert Hamerton-Kelly. Stanford: Stanford University Press.

Martin, Troy W. 2006. "Paul's Pneumatological Statements and Ancient Medical Texts." In *The New Testament and Early Christian Literature in Greco-Roman Context: Studies in Honor of David E. Aune*, edited by John Fotopoulos, 105–126. Leiden: Brill.

May, Gerhard. 1994. Creatio Ex Nihilo: The Doctrine of "Creation out of Nothing" in Early Christian Thought. Edinburgh: T&T Clark.

Meerson, Michael. 2013. "Rites of Passage in Magic and Mysticism." In *Hekhalot Literature in Context*, Boustan, Ra'anan, Martha Himmelfarb, and Peter Schäfer, 323–347. Tübingen: Mohr Siebeck.

Mertz, Elizabeth. 2007. "Semiotic Anthropology." *Annual Review of Anthropology* 36: 337–353.

Meshel, Zeev. 2012. Kuntillet Ajrud (Horvat Teman): An Iron Age II Religious Site on the Judah-Sinai Border. Jerusalem: Israel Exploration Society.

Mettinger, Tryggve N. D. 1982. The Dethronement of Sabaoth: Studies in the Shem and Kabod Theologies. Lund: CWK Gleerup.

Mettinger, Tryggve N. D. 2006. "A Conversation with My Critics: Cultic Images or Aniconism in the First Temple?" In *Essays on Ancient Israel in Its Near Eastern Context*, edited by Yairah Amit, Ehud Ben Zvi, Israel Finkelstein, and Oded Lipschits, 273–296. Winona Lake: Eisenbrauns.

Milgrom, Jacob. 1999. "The Case of the Suspected Adultress, Numbers 5:11–31: Redaction and Meaning." In *Women in the Bible: A Reader*, edited by Alice Bach, 475–482. New York: Routledge.

Mizrachi, Noam. 2009. "The Supposed Relationship between the Songs of the Sabbath Sacrifice and Hekhalot Literature: Linguistic and Stylistic Aspects [in Hebrew]." *Megillot: Studies in the Dead Sea Scrolls* 7: 263–298.

Mizrachi, Noam. 2015. "Priests of Qoreb: Linguistic Enigma and Social Code in the Songs of the Sabbath Sacrifice." In *Hebrew of the Late Second Temple Period*, edited by Eibert J. C. Tigchelaar and Pierre van Hecke, 37–64. Leiden: Brill.

Moore, Stephen, and Janice Anderson. 1998. "Taking It Like a Man." *Journal of Biblical Literature* 117(2): 249–273.

NPS (National Park Service). 2021. Leaving Tributes at the Vietnam Veterans Memorial. https://www.nps.gov/vive/learn/collections.htm. Accessed June 20, 2021.

Nehamas, Alexander. 1992. "Voices of Silence: On Gregory Vlastos' Socrates." *Arion* 2: 157–186.

Newsom, Carol. 1985. Songs of the Sabbath Sacrifice: A Critical Edition. Atlanta: Scholars Press.

Newsom, Carol. 1990. "'Sectually-Explicit' Literature from Qumran." In *The Hebrew Bible and Its Interpreters*, edited by William H. C. Propp, Baruch Halpern and David Noel Freedman, 167–187. Winona Lake: Eisenbrauns.

Niehoff, Maren. 2001. *Philo on Jewish Identity and Culture*. Texts and Studies in Ancient Judaism = Texte und Studien Zum Antiken Judentum, 86. Tübingen: Mohr Siebeck.

Niehoff, Maren. 2006. "Creatio Ex Nihilo Theology in Genesis Rabbah in Light of Christian Exegesis." *Harvard Theological Review* 99: 37–64.

Niehr, H. 1997. "In Search of YHWH's Cult Statue in the First Temple." In *The Image and the Book: Iconic Cults, Aniconism, and the Rise of Book Religion in Israel and the Ancient Near East*, edited by Karel van der Toorn, 73–95. Leuven: Uitgeverij Peeters.

Nitzan, Bilha. 1994. "Harmonic and Mystical Characteristics in Poetic and Liturgical Writings from Qumran." *Jewish Quarterly Review* 85: 163–183.

Nock, Arthur Darby. 1951. "Review of Meecham's Epistle to Diognetus." *Journal of Religion* 31: 214–216.

Noveroske-Tritten, Linda. 2015. "Bodies at Burning Man: Heterotopia, Temporality, and the Creative Act As Embodied Revolution." Ph.D. Thesis. University of California, Davis.

Olster, David. 1994. "Byzantine Hermeneutics after Iconoclasm: Word and Image in the Leo Bible." *Byzantion: Revue International Des Etudes Byzantines* 64: 419–458.

Olyan, Saul M. 1988. *Asherah and the Cult of Yahweh in Israel*. Atlanta: Scholars Press.

Parmentier, Richard. 1993. "The Political Function of Reported Speech: A Belauan Example." In *Reflexive Language and the Human Disciplines*, edited by John Lucy, 261–286. Cambridge: Cambridge University Press.

Parmentier, Richard. 1994. *Signs in Society: Studies in Semiotic Anthropology*. Bloomington: Indiana University Press.

Parmentier, Richard. 1997. "The Pragmatic Semiotics of Cultures." Semiotica: Journal of the International Association for Semiotic Studies/Revue de l'Association Internationale de Sémiotique 116: 1–115.

Parmentier, Richard. 2009. "Troubles with Trichotomies: Reflections on the Utility of Peirce's Sign Trichotomies for Social Analysis." *Semiotica* 177: 139–155.

Paul, Robert A. 1996. *Moses and Civilization: The Meaning behind Freud's Myth*. New Haven: Yale University Press.

Pearson, Birger A. 2007. *Ancient Gnosticism : Traditions and Literature*. Minneapolis: Fortress Press.

Penabaz, L. Gabrielle. 2014. "Engaging the Encouraging Priestess or Self-Marriage Becomes You in the Dust." In *Playa Dust*, edited by Samantha Krukowski, 120–129. London: Black Dog Publishing.

Penner, Hans. 1989. Impasse and Resolution: A Critique of the Study of Religion. New York: Peter Lang.

Philo. 1929–1953. F. H. Colson, G. H. Whitaker, and Ralph Marcus, trans. 9 vols. + 2 suppl. LCL. Cambridge: Harvard University Press.

Pike, Sarah. 2005. "No Novenas for the Dead: Ritual Action and Communal Memory at the Temple of Tears." In *Afterburn: Reflections on Burning Man*, edited by Lee Gilmore and Mark Van Proyen, 195–213. Albuquerque: University of New Mexico Press.

Pinakothek Bueys Multiples. 2021. What are multiples? https://pinakothek-beuys-multiples. de/what-are-multiples/?lang=en. Accessed June 20, 2021.

Principe, Walter. 1983. "Toward Defining Spirituality." *Studies in Religion* 12(2): 127–141.

Proudfoot, Wayne. 1985. *Religious Experience*. Berkeley: University of California Press.

Quack, Johannes. 2010. "Bell, Bourdieu, and Wittgenstein on Ritual Sense." In *The Problem of Ritual Efficacy*, edited by William Sax, Johannes Quack, and Jan Weinhold, 169–188. Oxford: Oxford University Press.

Raiser, Jennifer. 2016. *Burning Man: Art on Fire*. New York: Race Point Publishing.

Rappaport, Roy A. 1999. *Ritual and Religion in the Making of Humanity*. Cambridge Studies in Social and Cultural Anthropology 110. Cambridge, U.K.; New York: Cambridge University Press.

Remes, Pauliina. 2008. *Neoplatonism*. Berkeley: University of California Press.

Richter, Sandra L. 2002. *The Deuteronomistic History and the Name Theology: Lešakkēn Šemô Šām in the Bible and the Ancient Near East*. Beihefte Zur Zeitschrift Für Die Alttestamentliche Wissenschaft, Bd 318. Berlin; New York: Walter De Gruyter.

Ries, Julien. 1987. "Idolatry." In *Encyclopedia of Religion*, edited by Mircea Eliade, 7:72–81. New York: Macmillan.

Rist, John M. 1967. *Plotinus: The Road to Reality*. Cambridge: Cambridge University Press.

Robbins, Joel. 2001. "Ritual Communication and Linguistic Ideology: A Reading and Partial Reformulation of Rappaport's Theory of Ritual." *Current Anthropology* 42: 591–614.

Robertson, Paul. 2014. "De-Spiritualizing Pneuma: Modernity, Religion, and Anachronism in the Study of Paul." *Method and Theory in the Study of Religion* 26: 365–383.

Rosaldo, Michelle. 1982. "The Things We Do With Words: Ilongot Speech Acts and Speech Act Theory in Philosophy." *Language in Society* 11: 203–237.

Runia, David. 1988. "Naming and Knowing: Themes in Philonic Theology with Special Reference to De Mutatione Nominum." In *Knowledge of God in the Graeco-Roman World*, edited by Roel B. van den Broek, 69–91. Leiden: Brill.

Sanders, Seth. 2004. "Performative Utterances and Divine Language in Ugaritic." *Journal of Near Eastern Studies* 63(3): 161–181.

Sankin, Aaron. 2015. "Inside the Universal Life Church, the Internet's One True Religion." The Week, April 3, 2015. Version archived at https://www.academia.edu/32740102/Inside_ the_Universal_Life_Church_the_Internets_One_True_Religion, accessed January 6, 2022.

Satlow, Michael. 1996. "'Try to Be a Man': The Rabbinic Construction of Masculinity." *Harvard Theological Review* 89: 18–40.

Sauer, Eberhard. 2014. "Disabling Demonic Images: Regional Diversity in Ancient Iconoclasts' Motives and Targets." In *Iconoclasm from Antiquity to Modernity*, edited by Kristine Kolrud and Marina Prusac, 15–40. Burlington: Ashgate.

Schäfer, Peter. 1988. "The Problem of the Redactional Identity of Hekhalot Rabbati." In *Hekhalot-Studien*, Peter Schäfer, 63–74. Tübingen: Mohr.

Schäfer, Peter. 1992. The Hidden and Manifest God: Some Major Themes in Early Jewish Mysticism. Albany: State University of New York Press.

Schäfer, Peter. 1996. "Jewish Liturgy and Magic." In *Geschichte-Tradition-Reflexion*, edited by Peter Schäfer, 541–555. Tübingen: Mohr.

Schäfer, Peter. 2002. "The Triumph of Pure Spirituality: Sigmund Freud's Moses and Monotheism." *Jewish Studies Quarterly* 9: 381–406.

Schäfer, Peter, Margarete Schlüter, and Hans-Georg von Mutius. 1981. *Synopse Zur Hekhalot-Literatur*. Tübingen: Mohr.

Schaudig, Hanspeter. 2012. "Death of Statues and Rebirth of Gods." In *Iconoclasm and Text Destruction in the Ancient Near East and Beyond*, edited by Natalie N. May, 123–149. Chicago: Oriental Institute of Chicago.

Schechner, Richard. 1988. *Performance Theory*. Rev. and Expanded. New York: Routledge.

Schenk, Kara. 2010. "Temple, Community, and Sacred Narrative in the Dura-Europos Synagogue." *Association for Jewish Studies Review* 34: 195–229.

Schmidt, Brian. 2002. "The Iron Age Pithoi Drawings from Horvat Teman or Kuntillet Ajrud: Some New Proposals." *Journal of Ancient Near Eastern Religions* 2: 91–125.

Schmidt, Brian. 2016. The Materiality of Power : Explorations in the Social History of Early Israelite Magic. Tübingen: Mohr Siebeck.

Scholem, Gershom. 1960. *Jewish Gnosticism, Merkabah Mysticism, and Talmudic Tradition*. New York: Jewish Theological Seminary of America.

Scholem, Gershom. 1965. *On the Kabbalah and Its Symbolism*. New York: Schocken Books.

Schopen, Gregory. 1990. "On Monks, Nuns and 'Vulgar' Practices: The Introduction of the Image Cult into Indian Buddhism." *Artibus Asiae* 49: 153–168.

Schroeder, Frederic M. 1996. "Plotinus and Language." In *The Cambridge Companion to Plotinus*, edited by Lloyd Gerson, 336–355. Cambridge: Cambridge University Press.

Schroeder, Frederic M. 2002. "The Platonic Text as Oracle in Plotinus." In *Metaphysik Und Religion: Zur Signatur Des Spätantiken Denkens*, edited by Theo Kobusch and Michael Erler, 23–37. München: K.G. Saur.

Schuller, Eileen. 1999. "Hodayot." In *Qumran Cave 4.XX: Poetical and Liturgical Texts, Part 2*, DJD, 29:69–232. Oxford: Clarendon Press.

Searle, John R. 1969. *Speech Acts: An Essay in the Philosophy of Language*. London: Cambridge University Press.

Sedley, David. 1998. "The Etymologies in Plato's Cratylus." *Journal of Hellenic Studies* 118: 140–154.

Sedley, David. 2003. *Plato's Cratylus*. Cambridge Studies in the Dialogues of Plato. Cambridge, U.K.; New York: Cambridge University Press.

Sedley, David. 2007. *Creationism and Its Critics in Antiquity*. Berkeley: University of California.

Segert, Stanislav. 1988. "Observations on Poetic Structures in the Songs of the Sabbath Sacrifice." *Revue de Qumran* 13: 215–223.

Seligman, Adam B., and Robert P. Weller. 2012. *Rethinking Pluralism Ritual, Experience, and Ambiguity.* New York; Oxford: Oxford University Press,.

Sells, Michael. 1994. *Mystical Languages of Unsaying.* Chicago: University of Chicago.

Shister, Neil. 2019. Radical Ritual: How Burning Man Changed the World. Berkeley: Counterpoint.

Silverstein, Michael. 1976. "Shifters. Linguistic Categories and Cultural Descriptions." In *Meaning in Anthropology*, edited by Keith Basso and Henry Selby, 11–55. Albuquerque: University of New Mexico.

Silverstein, Michael. 1979. "Language Structure and Linguistic Ideology." In *The Elements*, edited by Paul Clyne, William Hanks, and Carol Hofhaur, 193–247. Chicago: Chicago Linguistic Society.

Silverstein, Michael. 1981. "Metaforces of Power in Traditional Oratory." https://www.scribd.com/document/47267680/Silverstein-Metaforces-of-Power.

Silverstein, Michael. 1993. "Metapragmatic Discourse and Metapragmatic Function." In *Reflexive Language: Reported Speech and Metapragmatics*, edited by John Lucy, 33–58. Cambridge: Cambridge University Press.

Silverstein, Michael. 1997. "The Improvisational Performance of Culture in Realtime Discursive Practice." In *Creativity in Performance*, edited by Keith Sawyer, 265–312. Greenwich: Ablex.

Silverstein, Michael. 1998. "The Uses and Utility of Ideology: A Commentary." In *Language Ideologies: Theory and Practice*, edited by Bambi B. Schieffelin, Kathryn A. Woolard, and Paul Kroskity, 123–45. New York: Oxford University Press.

Silverstein, Michael. 2000. "Whorfianism and the Linguistic Imagination of Nationality." In *Regimes of Language: Ideologies, Politics, and Identity*, edited by Paul Kroskity, 85–138. Santa Fe: School of American Research.

Silverstein, Michael. 2004. "'Cultural' Concepts and the Language-Culture Nexus." *Current Anthropology* 45: 621–652.

Silverstein, Michael. 2010. "'Direct' and 'Indirect' Communicative Acts in Semiotic Perspective." *Journal of Pragmatics* 42: 337–353.

Silverstein, Michael. 2016. "The Semiotic Varieties of Religious Experience." Presented at the Mediation and Immediacy: The Semiotic Turn in the Study of Religion, Torino, Italy, June 10.

Silverstein, Michael, and Greg Urban. 1996. *Natural Histories of Discourse.* Chicago: University of Chicago Press.

Smith, Imogen. 2014. "Taking the Tool Analogy Seriously: Forms and Naming in the Cratylus." *Cambridge Classical Journal* 60: 75–99.

Smith, Jonathan Z. 1978. Map Is Not Territory: Studies in the History of Religions. Leiden: Brill.

Smith, Jonathan Z. 1982. *Imagining Religion: From Babylon to Jonestown.* Chicago: University of Chicago Press.

Smith, Jonathan Z. 1987a. "The Domestication of Sacrifice." In *Violent Origins: Walter Burkert, René Girard, and Jonathan Z. Smith on Ritual Killing and Cultural Formation*, edited by Robert G. Hamerton-Kelly, 191–235. Stanford: Stanford University Press.

Smith, Jonathan Z. 1987b. *To Take Place: Towards Theory in Ritual*. Chicago: University of Chicago Press.

Smith, Jonathan Z. 2004. *Relating Religion: Essays in the Study of Religion*. Chicago; London: University of Chicago Press.

Smith, Morton. 1952. "The Common Theology of the Ancient Near East." *Journal of Biblical Theology* 71: 135–147.

Smith, Morton. 1963. "Observations on Hekhalot Rabbati." In *Biblical and Other Studies*, edited by Alexander Altmann, 142–160. Cambridge: Harvard University Press.

Smith, Morton. 1981. "Ascent to the Heavens and the Beginning of Christianity." *Eranos Jahrbuch* 50: 403–429.

Smith, Morton. 1983. "Transformation by Burial (1 Cor 15:35–49, Rom 6:3–5 and 8:9–11)." *Eranos* 52: 87–112.

Smith, Morton. 1990. "Ascent to the Heavens and Deification in 4MQa." In *Archaeology and History in the Dead Sea Scrolls*, edited by Lawrence Schiffman, 181–88. Sheffield: Sheffield Academic Press.

Sorabji, Richard. 1983. Time, Creation and the Continuum: Theories in Antiquity and the Early Middle Ages. London: Duckworth.

St. John, Graham. 2001. "Alternative Cultural Heterotopia and the Liminoid Body: Beyond Turner at ConFest." *Australian Journal of Anthropology* 12: 47–66.

Steiner, Deborah. 2001. Images in Mind: Statues in Archaic and Classical Greek Literature and Thought. Princeton: Princeton University Press.

Stevens, Richard. 2003. "Burning for the Other: Semiotics of a Levinasian Theological Aesthetics in Light of Burning Man." Ph.D. Thesis. Graduate Theological Union.

Strathern, Andrew. 1981. "'Noman': Representations of Identity in Mount Hagen." In *The Structure of Folk Models*, edited by Ladislav Holy and Milan Stuchlik, 281–303. London: Academic Press.

Stroumsa, Gedaliahu. 2005. "A Nameless God: Judaeo-Christian and Gnostic 'Theologies of the Name.'" In *Hidden Wisdom: Esoteric Traditions and the Roots of Christian Mysticism*, Gedaliahu Stroumsa, 184–199. Leiden: Brill.

Stroumsa, Gedaliahu. 2009. *The End of Sacrifice: Religious Transformations in Late Antiquity*. Chicago: University of Chicago Press.

Suter, Claudia. 2012. "Gudea of Lagash: Iconoclasm or Tooth of Time?" In *Iconoclasm and Text Destruction in the Ancient Near East and Beyond*, edited by Natalie May, 57–88. Chicago: Oriental Institute of Chicago.

Swartz, Michael D. 1994. "'Like the Ministering Angels': Ritual and Purity in Early Jewish Mysticism and Magic." *Association for Jewish Studies Review* 19: 135–167.

Swartz, Michael D. 2002. "Sacrificial Themes in Jewish Magic." In *Magic and Ritual in the Ancient World*, edited by Paul Mirecki and Marvin Meyer, 303–315. Leiden: Brill.

Tambiah, Stanley J. 1979. "A Performative Approach to Ritual." *Proceedings of the British Academy*, 65: 113–169.

Taylor, Mark C. 1998. *Critical Terms for Religious Studies*. Chicago: University of Chicago Press.

Tigay, Jeffrey H. 2013. "The Torah Scroll and God's Presence." In *Built by Wisdom, Established by Understanding*, edited by Maxine Grossman, 323–340. Bethesda: University Press of Maryland.

Tigchelaar, Eibert J. C. 1998. "Reconstructing 11Q17 Shirot 'Olat Ha-Shabbat." In *The Provo International Conference on the Dead Sea Scrolls*, 171–185. Leiden: Brill.

van der Toorn, Karel. 1990. "The Nature of the Biblical Teraphim in the Light of Cuneiform Evidence." *Catholic Biblical Quarterly* 52: 203–222.

van der Toorn, Karel. 1997. "The Iconic Book: Analogies between the Babylonian Cult of Images and the Veneration of the Torah." In *The Image and the Book: Iconic Cults, Aniconism, and the Religion in Israel and the Ancient Near East*, edited by Kael van der Toorn, 229–248. Leuven: Uitgeverij Peeters.

Tugendhaft, Aaron. 2012. "Images and the Political: On Jan Assmann's Concept of Idolatry." *Method and Theory in the Study of Religion* 24: 301–306.

Turner, Frederick Jackson. 1920. *The Frontier in American History*. New York: H. Holt and Company.

Turner, John. 1992. "Gnosticism and Platonism." In *Neoplatonism and Gnosticism*, edited by Richard T. Wallis and Jay Bregman, 425–459. Albany: State University of New York.

Turner, Victor W. 1979. *Process, Performance, and Pilgrimage: A Study in Comparative Symbology*. Ranchi Anthropology Series 1. New Delhi: Concept.

Uehlinger, Christoph. 1997. "Anthropomorphic Cult Statuary in Iron Age Palestine and the Search for Yahweh's Cult Images." In *The Image and the Book: Iconic Cults, Aniconism, and the Rise of Book Religion in Israel and the Ancient Near East*, edited by Karel van der Toorn, 97–155. Leuven: Uitgerverij Peeters.

Urban, Greg. 1991. A Discourse-Centered Approach to Culture: Native South American Myths and Rituals. Austin: University of Texas Press.

Urban, Hugh B. 2003. Tantra Sex, Secrecy Politics, and Power in the Study of Religions. Berkeley: University of California Press.

Urban, Hugh B. 2006. "Fair Game: Secrecy, Security, and the Church of Scientology in Cold War America." *Journal of the American Academy of Religion* 74: 356–389.

Valeri, Valerio. 1985. *Kingship and Sacrifice: Ritual and Society in Ancient Hawaii*. Chicago: University of Chicago Press.

van der Toorn, Karel. 2002. "Israelite Figurines: A View from the Texts." In *Sacred Time, Sacred Place: Archaeology and the Religion of Israel*, edited by Barry Gittlen, 45–62. Winona Lake: Eisenbrauns.

Vasileiadis, Pavlos. 2014. "Aspects of Rendering the Sacred Tetragrammaton in Greek." *Open Theology* 1: 56–88.

Vidas, Moulie. 2013. "Hekhalot Literature, the Babylonian Academies, and the Tanna'im." In *Hekhalot Literature of Context*, 141–176. Tübingen: Mohr Siebeck.

Vout, Caroline. 2005. "Antinous, Archaeology and History." *Journal of Roman Studies* 95: 80–96.

Walker, Christopher, and Michael Dick. 1999. "The Induction of the Cult Image in Ancient Mesopotamia: The Mesopotamian Mīs Pî Ritual." In *Born in Heaven Made on Earth: The Making of the Cult Image in the Ancient Near East*, edited by Michael Dick, 55–121. Winona Lake: Eisenbrauns.

Waugh, Linda. 1980. "The Poetic Function in the Theory of Roman Jakobson." *Poetics Today* 2: 57–82.

Weitzman, Steven. 2005. *Surviving Sacrilege: Cultural Persistence in Jewish Antiquity*. Cambridge: Harvard University Press.

Weitzmann, Kurt, and Herbert L. Kessler. 1990. *The Frescoes of the Dura Synagogue and Christian Art.* Dumbarton Oaks Studies 28. Washington, D.C.: Dumbarton Oaks Research Library and Collection.

Wheelock, Wade. 1982. "The Problem of Ritual Language: From Information to Situation." *Journal of the American Academy of Religion* 50: 49–71.

Whittaker, John. 1969. "Basilides on the Ineffability of God." *Harvard Theological Review* 62: 367–371.

Whittaker, John. 1983. "Arretos Kai Akatanomostos." In *Platonismus Und Christentum: Festschrift für H. Dorrie,* edited by Horst-Dieter Blume, 303–306. Münster: Aschendorff.

Whittaker, John. 1992. "Catachresis and Negative Theology: Philo of Alexandria and Basilides." In *Platonism in Late Antiquity,* edited by Stephen Gersh and Charles Kannengiesser, 61–82. Notre Dame: University of Notre Dame Press.

Williams, Bernard. 1982. "Cratylus' Theory of Names and Its Refutation." In *Language and Logos: Studies in Ancient Greek Philosophy Presented to G.E.L. Owen,* edited by Malcolm Schofield and Martha Nussbaum, 83–93. Cambridge: Cambridge University Press.

Williams, Michael. 1992. "Higher Providence, Lower Providence and Fate." In *Neoplatonism and Gnosticism,* edited by Richard T. Wallis and Jay Bregman, 483–507. Albany: State University of New York.

Williams, Michael. 1996. Rethinking "Gnosticism": An Argument for Dismantling a Dubious Category. Princeton: Princeton University Press.

Winch, Peter. 1964. "Understanding a Primitive Society." *American Philosophical Quarterly* 1(4): 307–324.

Winnicott, Donald W. 1953. "Transitional Objects and Transitional Phenomena: A Study of the First Not-Me Possession." *International Journal of Psychoanalysis* 34: 89–97.

Winnicott, Donald W. 1971. *Playing and Reality.* New York: Basic Books.

Winston, David. 1971. "The Book of Wisdom's Theory of Cosmogony." *History of Religions* 11: 185–202.

Winston, David. 1991. "Aspects of Philo's Linguistic Theory." In *Heirs of the Septuagint: Philo, Hellenistic Judaism and Early Christianity,* edited by David T. Runia, David M. Hay, and David Winston, 109–125. Atlanta: Scholars Press.

Winter, Irene. 2000. "Opening the Eyes and Opening the Mouth: The Utility of Comparing Images in Worship in India and the Ancient Near East." In *Ethnography and Personhood: Notes from the Field,* edited by Michael W. Meister, 129–162. Jaipur and New Delhi: Rawat Publications.

Wolfson, Elliot. 1994. "Mysticism and the Poetic-Liturgical Compositions from Qumran: A Response to Bilhah Nitzan." *Jewish Quarterly Review* 85: 185–202.

Wolfson, Harry. 1948. Philo: Foundations of Religious Philosophy in Judaism, Christianity and Islam. Cambridge: Cambridge University Press.

Woods, Christopher. 2012. "Mutilation of Image and Text in Early Sumerian Sources." In *Iconoclasm and Text Destruction in the Ancient Near East and Beyond,* edited by Natalie N. May, 33–55. Chicago: Oriental Institute of Chicago.

Yadin, Yigael. 1962. The Scroll of the War of the Sons of Light against the Sons of Darkness. London: Oxford University Press.

Yelle, Robert A. 2016. "The Peircean Icon and the Study of Religion: A Brief Overview." *Material Religion* 12: 241–243.

Zwissler, Laurel. 2011. "Pagan Pilgrimage: New Religious Movements Research on Sacred Travel within Pagan and New Age Communities." *Religion Compass* 5: 326–342.

Index of Persons

https://doi.org/10.1515/9783110768602-012

Index of subjects

https://doi.org/10.1515/9783110768602-013

www.ingramcontent.com/pod-product-compliance
Lightning Source LLC
Chambersburg PA
CBHW021620270326
41931CB00008B/798